ENDORSEMENTS

A Transcendental Education provides a powerfully hopeful, integrative, and holistic vision that can help guide education out of its current vacuum. The book is thoughtfully explicated, expertly synthesized, and completely relevant for anyone interesting in helping education find itself. Like the transcendentalists themselves, this is both down-to-earth and soaring in its potential implications.

—Tobin Hart author of *"The Secret Spiritual World of Children"* and *"From Information to Transformation: Education for the Evolution of Consciousness."*

The secret to a vital, renewed America lies in the life and writings of the Transcendentalist community of Concord, Massachusetts in the 19th century. Jack Miller, who I know has been devoted to a new, living form of education throughout his career, has written a book that could inspire a revolution in teaching. It goes against the tide, as do Emerson and Thoreau. But it offers a blueprint and a hope for our children.

—Thomas Moore, author of *"Care of the Soul"*

A timely account of great thinking on genuine education. Reading this, today's beleaguered teachers should experience a renewal of spirit and commitment.

—Nel Noddings, author *of Happiness and Education.*

Transcendental Learning

The Educational Legacy of Alcott, Emerson, Fuller, Peabody and Thoreau

Transcendental Learning

The Educational Legacy of Alcott, Emerson, Fuller, Peabody and Thoreau

by

John P. Miller
University of Toronto

Information Age Publishing, Inc.
Charlotte, North Carolina • www.infoagepub.com

Library of Congress Cataloging-in-Publication Data

Transcendental learning : the educational legacy of Alcott, Emerson, Fuller, Peabody and Thoreau / edited by John P. Miller.
    p. cm.
  Includes bibliographical references.
  ISBN 978-1-61735-584-4 (pbk.) -- ISBN 978-1-61735-585-1 (hardcover) -- ISBN 978-1-61735-586-8 (ebook)
  1. Holistic education. 2. Transcendentalism. 3. Learning. I. Miller, John P., 1943-
  LC990.T73 2011
  370.15'23--dc23   2011031942

Printed in the United States of America

DEDICATION

To the memory of

Jean Marie Miller

My wife and mother of our children, Patrick and Nancy.

CONTENTS

PREFACE

It is not a man's duty as a matter of course, to devote himself to the eradication of any, even the most enormous wrong; he may still properly have other concerns to engage him; but it is his duty, at least to wash his hands of it.... If the injustice is part of the necessary friction of the machine of government, let it go ... but if it is of such nature that it requires you to be the agent of injustice to another, then I say, break the law.

—Thoreau

This quotation changed my life. As a draft-age American in the late 1960s, I struggled with the issue of the Vietnam war and what I would do if called. After reading about this conflict, I concluded it was a civil war amongst the Vietnamese people and that American intervention was wrong. If drafted, I would become "an agent of injustice" in an unjust war.... This experience began a long relation to the work of Thoreau and eventually all the people discussed in this book.

In 1969, I was drafted and my wife, Jean, and I decided to immigrate to Canada where I have lived ever since. I remember during the first year in Toronto, where I was studying at the Ontario Institute for Studies in Education, Jean and I listened to a reading of *Walden* on the radio in the evenings. In the early 1980s, I read a biography of Emerson by Gay Wilson Allen, which led me to read Emerson's essays, which I turn to frequently for inspiration and wisdom.

As an educator, the more I read and learned about Thoreau, Emerson, Alcott, Fuller, and Peabody, I realized they held a vision of education that today we term "holistic." Holistic education focuses on educating the whole person, or in the words of Gandhi—the head, hands, and heart. Gandhi also said these three form an indivisible whole and that if we just concentrate on one we commit a gross fallacy. Most departments of educations around the world have committed this fallacy with an emphasis on the intellect alone. The Transcendentalists, however, did not make this mistake and instead offer a more inclusive and inspiring vision of education.

Holistic education has deep roots going back to indigenous peoples. Greg Cajete in *Look to the Mountain* describes the basic principles of indigenous education and how they are deeply holistic and ecological. Holistic education can also be found in the great teachers of the Axial age described in Karen Armstrong's *The Great Transformation*. The central teaching of the Buddha, Socrates, Confucius, the Israeli prophets, and the mystics of the Upanishads saw human being as whole and capable of compassion for other beings. In the eighteenth century, Rousseau and Pestalozzi through their work also articulated a holistic vision of education. Rousseau's goal was to have the person "seeing with his own eyes, feeling with his own heart, and governed by no authority except his own reason" (Darmrosch, p. 334). For Rousseau, the important rule in education was not to "gain time, but to lose it"; an idea echoed in the Transcendentalist vision of learning.

The Transcendentalists, then, are part of long tradition that sees education as freeing the human being and at the same time helping the person become connected to the community, the earth and the universe. I believe in a time when we hear that education should be training students so they can compete in the global marketplace that we can benefit immensely from exploring the Transcendentalist vision of education. Given the challenges that face us today a economic approach to education will simply not suffice. We need an education for wisdom, and the Transcendentalist vision can inspire and help us in this important work.

REFERENCE

Damrosch, L. (2005). *Jean-Jacques Rousseau: Restless genius*. Boston: Houghton Mifflin.

ACKNOWLEDGEMENTS

I am grateful to Tobin Hart and Bruce Ronda who read and commented on earlier versions of the manuscript. I have tried to incorporate several of their suggestions in the book. Thanks also to Thomas Moore and Nel Noddings for reading the manuscript and writing supportive comments. I am also grateful to John Matteson for his encouraging remarks on the worthiness of pursuing a project regarding the Transcendentalists' views on education.

I want to express my gratitude to George Johnson and the staff at Information Age Publishing for all the work they have done on the production of *Transcendental Learning*. I was particularly appreciative of how responsive George was to my queries and the speediness of the production process.

Finally, arigato to my wife, Midori, who carefully read and corrected the page proofs.

CHAPTER 1

A TRANSCENDENTAL EDUCATION

We shall one day learn to supersede politics by education. What we call our root-and-branch reforms of slavery, war, gambling, intemperance, is only medicating the symptoms. We must begin higher up, namely, in Education.

—Emerson

In antebellum America, a group of individuals living mostly in Concord Massachusetts have had a continuing influence on our lives. Daniel Walker Howe in his Pulitzer Prize winning history of the antebellum period in America, *What Hath God Wrought*, writes about the "extraordinary outburst of genius" which was comparable to fifth century Athens or sixteenth century Florence. Howe (2007) also writes of their continuing impact:

> The writings of the Transcendentalists affirm some of the best qualities characteristic of American civilization: self-reliance, willingness to question authority, a quest for spiritual nourishment. Their writings, even today, urge us to independent reflection in the face of fads, conformity, blind partisanship, and mindless consumerism. (p. 626)

It is somewhat ironic that a movement that focused on the individual could impact social and political movements including the independence of India and the civil rights movement in the United States. In *Blessed Unrest*, Paul Hawken argues that Emerson's ideas formed a seed that grew through the work of Thoreau, Gandhi, and Martin Luther King. Hawken writes that when Emerson came to France in 1832, he was moved by his visits to the Jardin des Plantes and the Cabinet of Natural History in Paris. Walking in the Jardin des Plantes and seeing how animals and nature were connected led Emerson to his insight of how life was deeply interconnected. He wrote later, "Nature is intricate, overlapped, interweaved, and endless" (Emerson, 2003, p. 433). Hawken (2007) writes, "It was Emerson's first encounter with the web of life" (p. 73). This insight led Emerson to write his essay *Nature* which became one of the key works in Transcendentalism. Emerson "planted seeds that would develop into what were, and continue to be, two disparate concepts that animate our daily existence: how we treat nature and how we treat one another—the foundations of environmental and social justice" (p. 73). To support this assertion, Hawken cites Emerson: "I have confidence in laws of morals as of botany. I have planted maize in my field every June for 17 years and I never knew it to come up strychnine. My parsley, beet, turnip, carrot, buckthorn, and acorn, are as sure. I believe that just produces justice, and injustice injustice" (Hawken, pp. 73–74).

Thoreau picked up these two strands which bore fruit in *Walden,* a book that continues to inspire the environmental movement and *Civil Disobedience* which Gandhi read in 1906. When Gandhi was first arrested in South Africa in 1908, he took Thoreau's writings with him so he "could find arguments in favor of our fight" (p. 79). It was Thoreau's integration of ideas and practice that appealed to Gandhi. For Gandhi, Thoreau was someone who "taught nothing he was not prepared to practice himself" (Gandhi, p. 113). This was something that Gandhi took to heart and when asked once about giving some words of wisdom he said that "my life is my message."

In 1956, during the Montgomery bus boycott a colleague gave Martin Luther King three books: Gandhi's *Autobiography,* Thoreau's *Civil Disobedience*, and Richard Gregg's *The Power of Non Violence*. When the boycott was finished and King was asked what books influenced him the most he mentioned all three of these works. Today, the Dalai Lama and Aung San Suu Kyi in Burma continue to echo the original message of Emerson and Thoreau with their nonviolent ethic.

As Paul Hawken (2007) has so ably documented, this vision has continued today particularly through the nonviolence ethic but also through what he refers to as the "movement without a name." This is a movement that includes perhaps two million grass roots groups around the world working for constructive change. The core ethic that unites these groups is rooted in the ethic of nonviolence and a sense of the sacred.

In education, this movement includes a diverse group including Waldorf, Montessori, Reggio Emilia schools, home schooling, democratic schools, and varieties of alternative approaches to education. These educators tend to embrace a vision of educating the whole child and reject the mechanistic models that currently dominate the educational scene. In Toronto, for example, a group of parents, community members, and teachers have come together to initiate a school for the whole child within the Toronto District School Board (www.wholechildschool.ca) that started in September 2009 (Miller, 2010). This school is now called Equinox Holistic Alternative School and incorporates some of the features of Transcendental Learning.

The Transcendentalists were interested in education but unlike the work I have just discussed, we have ignored their vision of learning. It is high time that we looked more closely at their view of teaching and learning. Alcott and Peabody devoted their lives to teaching and learning but Emerson, Fuller, and Thoreau also taught and shared many thoughts on education. The thesis of this book is that they left an important legacy that can help us move beyond today's narrow view of education that focuses on preparing students so that they can compete in the global economy. What we have today is education that centers on job creation and high stakes testing that is part of a corporate view of schooling. Emerson's (1966) critique of education still holds today. He wrote about what we fail to give students.

> We do not give them training as if we believed in their noble nature. We scarce educate their bodies. We do not train the eye and the hand. We exercise their understandings to the apprehension and comparison of some facts, to a skill in numbers in words; we aim to make accountants, attorneys, engineers, but not to make able, earnest, great-hearted men. (p. 211)

For the past 25 years educational reform has focused on testing as the way to improve student achievement. No Child Left Behind (NCLB) has been the culminating legislation of this movement in the United States. In her book *Tested*, Linda Perlstein provides a dispassionate account of how one school in Maryland has coped with the demands of NCLB. Her account describes a school day that is almost entirely devoted to preparing for the Maryland School Assessment Test (MSA) which is administered in March. Here is a typical day

8:45–10 Mock MSA
10–11:40 Identify tone in a poem. Identify the importance of advertisements.
 Review parts of speech
11:40–12:20 Lunch and recess
12:30–1:50 Language Arts
1:50–2:25 Summary of a fiction text. (p. 179)

Teachers complain that there is little time for subjects such as science and social studies. The arts are marginalized. This curriculum makes no attempt to educate the whole child. Compare this approach to Gandhi's (1980) conception of education

> I hold that true education of the intellect can only come through a proper exercise and training of the bodily organs, for example, hands, feet, eyes, ears, nose, etc. In other words, an intelligent use of the bodily organs in a child provides the best and quickest way of developing his intellect. But unless the development of the mind and body goes hand in hand with a corresponding awakening of the soul, the former alone would prove to be a poor lopsided affair. By spiritual training I mean education of the heart. A proper and all round development of the mind, therefore, can take place only when it proceeds *pari passu* with the education of the physical and spiritual faculties of the child. They constitute an indivisible whole. According to this theory, therefore, it would be a gross fallacy to suppose that they can be developed piecemeal or independently of one another. (p. 138)

Unfortunately, rather than following Gandhi's vision, departments and ministries of education in most countries have followed the piecemeal approach and the result has been disastrous. Education systems have reinforced fragmentation rather than connectedness. They have become part of a world where there is corporate corruption, deep distrust of politicians and the political process, environmental destruction, and an empty lifestyle based on materialism and consumption. The obsession with test results rather than a sensible approach to accountability has only led to deeper and more pervasive forms of fragmentation and alienation. In the fall of 2008, the world experienced a financial meltdown that began in the United States where investment banks and the banking system in general were engaged in high-risk investment strategies. Many of the individuals running these institutions were educated in the best universities in the U.S. Clearly, there was little wisdom in their decisions that led to the financial mess. We also live in a world where each day there is more evidence of climate change that could very soon make much of the world uninhabitable. Yet, governments and world leaders refuse to seriously address the problem.

In contrast to the current vision schooling, the Transcendentalists offer an inspiring vision of education that focuses on wholeness and wisdom. Its aim, as Emerson states, is to produce "great-hearted" individuals. It does not deny the spiritual and provides a language and approach to spirituality that is inclusive.

WHAT WAS TRANSCENDENTALISM?

Most of the people who are identified with the word transcendentalism did not use this word much or refer to themselves as part of a movement. They tended to be very individualistic and not oriented to group endeavors. Still Emerson did write an essay on Transcendentalism and the name stuck.

The Transcendentalists argued for a nondogmatic and more universalistic perspective that still resonates today. Buell (2006) notes that they were the first group of American thinkers who seriously examined nonwestern spiritual traditions including Hinduism and Buddhism. Both Emerson and Thoreau read the *Bhagavad-Gita*; Paul Friedrich (2008) has recently written book on *The Gita within Walden*. Emerson wrote, "Can anyone doubt that if the noblest saint among the Buddhists, the noblest Mahometan, the highest Stoic of Athens, the purest and wisest Christian, M[a]nu in India, Confucius in China, Spinoza in Holland, could somewhere meet and converse together, they would find themselves of one religion?" (Buell, p. xx). Gandhi (1980) echoed the same idea when he stated "The forms are many, but the informing spirit is one. How can there be room for distinctions of high and low where there is this all-embracing fundamental unity underlying the outward diversity? For that is a fact meeting you at every step in daily life. The final goal of all religions is to realize this essential oneness" (p. 63). Emerson and Gandhi are referring to what some have called the perennial philosophy or what Jorge Ferrer calls a "Relaxed Universalism" which acknowledges both unity and diversity. Post-modernism has not looked favorably on articulating universalistic perspectives, but as Buell argues that without some sense of common perspective "the United Nations.... Universal Declaration of Human Rights would never have seen the light of day" (p. xxi). While we must recognize the importance of diversity, we also need to acknowledge what we share as human beings. As the Dalai Lama has noted, this acknowledgment is the basic source of compassion.

Soul was central to Transcendentalism. Emerson (2003) constantly referred to the soul in his work. Some of his thoughts on the soul include:

"The one thing in the world, of value, is the active soul." (p. 230)
"The soul invites every man to expand to the full circle of the universe, and will have no preferences but those of spontaneous love." (p. 253)
"The Universe is the externization of the soul." (p. 332)
"They think society wiser than their soul, and know not the one soul and their soul, is wiser than the whole world." (p. 261)

This idea that the ultimate reference point is the soul has been articulated before in various religious and philosophical traditions. Socrates referred to the inner "daemon" and Christ to the "kingdom of God within." Hindus call this place the Atman and Buddhists refer to our Buddha Nature. This concept of an unconditioned self, or soul, is a core idea that Emerson's conversation of sages would assent to.

As noted above, this focus on the light within each individual led to social and political change. Besides the thread of nonviolence there was also other changes including a call for gender equality, primarily through the voice of Margaret Fuller (see Chapter 4). Some Transcendentalists such as Ripley, Orestes Brownson, and Theodore Parker focused on social change and social justice. Much of this activity focused on the abolition of slavery which also enlisted the energy of Emerson and Thoreau.

Fuller, Bronson Alcott, and Elizabeth Peabody also called for educational reform that moved away for an authoritarian and transmission approach to education to a more holistic vision. It is the core thesis of this book that the Transcendentalists provide a vision of education that is worth examining today. Holistic education, which in the words of Gandhi focuses on educating the head, hands, and heart, is sometimes associated with New Age thinking. This ignores the roots of holistic education which can be taken back to the axial age (Armstrong, 2006) and indigenous cultures. Lawrence Buell who has written extensively on the Transcendentalists suggests that three principal figures were Emerson, Thoreau, and Fuller. In this book, I discuss each of these individuals as well as a Bronson Alcott, and Elizabeth Peabody.

In contrast to the narrow vision of education that is promoted by governments and the media, the Transcendentalists offer a redemptive vision of education that includes the following:

- *educating the whole child-body, mind, and soul;*
- *happiness as a goal of education;*
- *educating students so they see the interconnectedness in nature;*
- *recognizing the inner wisdom of the child as something to be honored and nurtured;*
- *a blueprint for environmental education through the work of Thoreau;*
- *an inspiring vision for educating women of all ages through the work of Fuller;*
- *an experimental approach to pedagogy that continually seeks for more effective ways of educating children;*
- *a recognition of the importance of the presence of teacher and encouraging teachers to be aware and conscious of their own behavior;and*
- *a vision of multicultural and bilingual education through the work of Elizabeth Peabody.*

The Transcendentalists challenge us to provide an education that inspires or, in Emerson's words, sets "the hearts of youth on flame." Transcendental education recognizes what Thoreau (2002) said that " Surely joy is the condition of life" (p. 5).

Transcendental learning engages the child fully; of course, not every moment in a Transcendental classroom is an epiphany but ultimately students look forward to coming to schools that employ the principles outlined by the Transcendentalists.

THE CONTEXT

Transcendentalism arose in antebellum America. Daniel Walker Howe in his Pulitzer prize winning history of this period, *What Hath God Wrought: The Transformation of America 1815–1848* describes a period of territorial expansion, rapid population growth as well as social, economic, and social change. The two main technological changes were the rise of the railroad, which facilitated travel across the eastern part of the United States and the telegraph. At the beginning of this period, it took 19 days to travel from New York to Cincinnati but by 1848 the travel time by train was about three days.

Life was harsh. People rarely bathed and as late as 1832 a New England country doctor complained that four out of five of his patients did not bath from one year to the next. It was an agrarian society and "with an outlook more entrepreneurial than peasant" as the farmer bought more land than he could cultivate in hopes that its value would grow with the increasing population. The farmer as well as other members of society tended towards a Jeffersonian view of the world with an emphasis on individual liberty with respect to economic endeavors. Religion, however, was the counter to this individualism as people saw themselves as being part of a church community. In New England, this tendency followed in the tradition of the Puritans who would meet in Congregational meeting house.

Howe summarizes what America was like when he writes:

> The United States in 1815 resembled the economically developing countries of today in many ways: high birthrate, rapid population growth, most people being in the agricultural sector and surplus rural population migrating in quest of a livelihood. Poor transportation meant that many farms in the hinterland operated only just above subsistence level.... Save in New England, free public education represented the exception rather than the rule. (p. 43)

As noted, religion was powerful force. This was the period of "Second Great Awakening." Howe (2007) argues that the focus on being seen equal in the eyes of God was generally empowering. "Including women, the poor, and African Americans among the exhorters and exhorted, the revivals expanded the number of people experiencing an autonomous sense of self. They taught self-respect and demanded that individuals function as moral agents. In this way, the Awakening empowered multitudes" (p. 188).

Politically, this period began as the "Era of Good Feeling" when political parties were seen as problematic. Of course, the good feeling did not endure as parties arose with the two dominant parties at the end of the period being the Democrats and the Whigs. Only men could vote but they were very engaged and the election of 1840 had a massive turnout of 80.2% of the electorate. Howe asserts, "We should not read the current political apathy of the American public back into the antebellum past. The public was not yet jaded then" (p. 577). Slavery became the central political issue during this time and the Transcendentalists become more and more involved in speaking against it.

Educationally, there was a growth in the number of colleges, which grew from 33 in 1815 to 113 in 1848. Most of these (88) were Protestant denominational colleges. Another important development by mid-century was the increasing number of colleges for women so that by 1880 one third of all American students enrolled in higher education were female. This was unique in the world.

Howe notes that a main feature of the colleges was a course in moral philosophy taught to seniors by the president of the college. "The capstone of an undergraduate education, it treated not only the branch of philosophy we call ethical theory but also psychology and all the other social sciences, approached from a normative point of view. The dominant school of thought was that of the Scottish philosophers of "common sense," Thomas Reid and Dugald Stewart" (p. 463).

At the beginning of this period it was only in New England that communities supported a public, or common school. In the rest of the United States, education came through churches. The Sunday school provided 1 day week of instruction in basic literacy for 200,000 American children in 1827. Of course, the pedagogy focused mostly on recitation and rote learning.

The husband of Mary Peabody, Elizabeth's sister, Horace Mann was instrumental in the growth of public education. However, his vision was not congruent with the Transcendentalists. Bickman's (2003) citation of Mann is revealing: "It is well, when the wise and learned discover new truths; but how much better to diffuse the truths already discovered, amongst the multitude!.... Diffusion, then, rather than discovery, is the duty of our government" (p. 5). Bickman describes the components of schooling which Mann supported and to large extent still exist today, "the grouping of students by age in self-contained classrooms with a single teacher; the division knowledge into "subjects"; the use of textbooks to teach these subjects; the exclusive reliance on paper-and-pencil test to measure knowledge; and the production of regular report cards to disseminate these measurements" (p. 8). The Transcendental and holistic vision of education has remained on the margins, and today like the individuals discussed in this book we struggle to develop an approach to education that is truly life affirming.

Intellectual Roots of Transcendentalism

Transcendentalism had its roots in Unitarianism and German Idealism. Unitarianism rejected the Calvinist view that humans were born in original sin. William Ellery Channing (2006), a charismatic Unitarian Minister, in essay entitled "Humanity's Likeness to God" wrote that humans can "approach and resemble the mind of God" (p. 13). "God is another name for human intelligence, raised above all error and imperfection, and extended to all possible truth" (p. 15). Howe (2007) writes, "Channing's philosophy is best characterized as a form of Christian humanism." He also "added an Enlightenment faith in individual rights and in reasoning from empirical evidence similar to that of most other American Protestants" (pp. 614–615). Channing was a mentor to Elizabeth Peabody and this relationship is described in more detail in Chapter 6. Howe also notes that the impact of Unitarianism on education in the United States:

"Encouraging a view of education as a process of development rather than discipline, Unitarianism produced disproportionate number of American Educators as well as writers and reformers involved in the anti-slavery and women's rights movements" (p. 617).

This period in American history was also characterized by millennialism where people saw themselves "initiating a new order of the ages, democratic and free, in harmony with the divine." Transcendentalism was caught up in this same vision but was more removed from the religious overtones connected to other millennial projects.

The other source was German Idealism, which rejected John Locke's empiricism which was too materialistic for the Transcendentalists. Instead, they turned to Kant and one of his interpreters, Samuel Coleridge, who made the distinction between "Reason" or divine intuition and "Understanding" or inductive reasoning (Buell, p. xix). Coleridge (2006) articulated an ancient notion that the way to deeper insight is through contemplation or what he called an "inward Beholding" (p. 10).

Frederic Henry Hedge, George Ripley, and Oresetes Brownson were among the first individuals who were involved in Transcendentalism that were influenced by German thought. Hedge studied German so he could read the German philosophers in their native tongue. He wrote an essay on Coleridge that had an immediate impact. It was Hedge, who also organized the meetings of the Transcendentalists that eventually included Alcott, Channing, Emerson, Fuller, Peabody, Thoreau, and others. The first meeting was held in 1836 in Cambridge and these gatherings lasted for 4 years and were referred to as Hedge's club.

George Ripley, who was editor of the *The Christian Examiner,* introduced his readers to German thought, particularly the work of the Friedrich Schleiermacher who "reconciled the conflicting claims of religion and science by clarifying the essential character of the former" (Gura, p. 66). Ripley has provided one of the best descriptions of the core principles of Transcendentalism.

There is a class of persons who desire a reform in the prevailing philosophy of the day. These are called Transcendentalists, because they believe in an order of truths which transcends the sphere of the external senses. Their leading idea is the supremacy of mind over matter. Hence, they maintain that the truth of religion does not depend on tradition, or on historical facts, but has

an unerring witness in the soul. There is a light, they believe, which enlight-
eneth every man that cometh in to the world; there is a faculty in all the most
degraded, the most ignorant, the most obscure, to perceive spiritual truth,
when distinctly repented; and the ultimate appeal, on all moral questions, is
not to a jury of scholars, hierarchy of divines, or the prescriptions of a creed,
but to the common sense of the race. (Gura, p. 143)

Brownson also contributed essays on Schleiermacher to the *Examiner.*
Later in his life he converted to Catholicism but in these years he was a
member of the Hedge club. Gura (2007) in his history of Transcendentalism argues that Brownson and Ripley, who were close friends, were the "de
facto generals of the emergent Transcendental movement, popularizing
Idealist thought through their seminal publications and applying it to
pressing social needs"(p. 75). Brownson like the other Transcendentalists
believed in a universal religious sentiment that was part of the soul and that
his sentiment was the ultimate source of insight and wisdom. He wrote in
his book *New Views of Christianity, Society and the Church* that "Humanity,
Nature, and God have precisely the same law, that what we find in nature
and Humanity we may also find in God" (Gura, p. 77).

Although Hedge, Ripley, and Brownson were instrumental in starting
the movement we call Transcendentalism, it is the individuals discussed in
this book that are most associated with the term. In particular, Emerson,
Fuller, and Thoreau are the names that most frequently connected with
Transcendentalism.

TRANCENDENTAL EDUCATORS

I have chosen to describe the work of the following five individuals because
they all taught at one time and held a view of education that was essentially
holistic.

Ralph Waldo Emerson

Ralph Waldo Emerson was the intellectual leader of the Transcendentalists and mentor to the others described in this book. His lectures and essays
inspired many individuals connected with Transcendentalism. Buell comments that for the Transcendentalists it was more important to "inspire
than explain" (p. xxiii). Emerson did not lay out a systematic philosophy
but wrote and spoke in a manner that moved the reader and the listener.
James Russell Lowell wrote "I have heard some great speakers and some
accomplished orators, but never any that so moved and persuaded me as
he" (cited in McAleer, p. 493). Many of Emerson's ideas resonate with a
holistic perspective. Emerson (1990) wrote "Nothing is quite beautiful

alone, nothing but is beautiful in the whole. A single object is only so far beautiful as it suggests this universal grace" (p. 26).

Henry David Thoreau

Henry David Thoreau lived in Concord and would stay in Emerson's home while Emerson was away lecturing. Thoreau was the earthy face of Transcendentalism. He loved nature and could be viewed as the father of the American environmental movement with his book *Walden* as one of its seminal texts. Thoreau was also a teacher; he and his brother, John, started and ran their own school that incorporated principles of holistic learning.

Margaret Fuller

Margaret Fuller can be viewed not only as one the foremost Transcendentalists but as one of the most important women in nineteenth century America. Her book, *Woman in the Nineteenth Century*, explored the intellectual and social position of women and argued against women's second class status. She was also the first editor of the journal of Transcendentalism, *The Dial*. Fuller was also an elementary school teacher but is most known for the "Conversations" that she ran for women in Boston. She led discussions with women that covered a wide range of topics that were designed to intellectually engage the women who participated. Howe (2007) writes that "From our standpoint in 21st century, the Transcendentalist who looks the most "modern" is Margaret Fuller. Versatile and passionate, she made her impact felt on journalism, feminism, criticism (literary, music, and art) and revolution" (p. 621). I would add education as well to this list.

Bronson Alcott

Bronson Alcott was interested in education throughout his life. He founded the Temple School in Boston where he engaged the students in discussions and inquiry that differed radically from the recitation and drill approach so common in most schools at that time. Alcott believed children held an inner wisdom that could be drawn out through Socratic questioning.

Elizabeth Peabody

Like Bronson Alcott, Elizabeth Peabody devoted her life to education. Bruce Ronda (1999) in his biography of Peabody states that "education was her great calling and her grand passion" (p. 7). She taught in several schools and helped Alcott in the Temple School, which she wrote about in *Record of a School*. Her crowning achievement was being an advocate for kindergarten. Having influenced by the work of Freidrich Froebel, Peabody argued that emphasis in kindergarten should be on play rather than academic work in the United States.

Gruenewald (2002) in an article on "Teaching and Learning with Thoreau" writes:

> I believe that the troubled profession of teaching could benefit greatly from taking seriously the kind of dissent, experimentation, and holistic living-in-place that Thoreau's legacy embodies. We may need him today more than ever before. So let us consider the ways in which we spend our lives, and let that reflection shape the kind of education we make possible for ourselves, and our students. (p. 539)

I would argue that not just Thoreau but the Transcendentalists discussed in this book deserve a more detailed exploration of their views on education and that is the aim of this text. In our day of factory-like models of schooling and it would be wise to reflect and re-imagine education from their ideas. This could help us today to develop a broader view of education that focuses on the development of whole human beings that can think, feel and act.

REFERENCES

Armstrong, K. (2006). *The great transformation: The beginning of our religious traditions.* New York, NY: Knopf.

Bickman, M. (2003). *Minding American education.* New York, NY: Teachers College Press.

Buell, L. (2006). "Introduction." In L. Buell (Ed.), *The American transcendentalists: Essential writings* (xi–xxiii). New York, NY: Penguin.

Channing, W. E. (2006). Humanity's likeness to God (1828). In L. Buell (Ed.), *The American transcendentalists: Essential writings* (11–15). New York, NY: Penguin.

Coleridge, S. T. (2006). Reason versus understanding (1825, 1829). In L. Buell (Ed.), *The American transcendentalists: Essential writings* (9–10). New York, NY: Penguin.

Emerson, R. W. (1966). Education. In H. M. Jones (Ed.), *Emerson on education: Selections.* New York, NY: Teachers College Press.

Emerson, R. W. (2003). *Selected writings of Ralph Waldo Emerson.* New York, NY: Signet.

Friedrich, P. (2008). *The Gita within Walden.* Albany, NY: SUNY Press.

Gandhi, M. (1980). *All men are brothers: Autobiographical reflections*, K. Kriplanai (Ed.). New York, NY: Continuum.

Gruenewald, D. A. (2002). Teaching and learning with Thoreau. *The Harvard Educational Review, 72*, 515–539.

Gura, P. F. (2007). *American transcendentalism: A history.* New York, NY: Hill and Wang.

Hawken, P. (2007). *Blessed unrest: How the largest movement in the world came into being and why no one saw it coming.* New York, NY: Viking.

Howe, D. W. (2007). *What Hath God Wrought: The transformation of America, 1815–1848.* New York: Oxford University Press.

McAleer, J. J. (1984). *Ralph Waldo Emerson: Days of Encounter.* Boston: Little, Brown.

Miller, J. (2010). *Whole child education.* Toronto: University of Toronto Press.

Perlstein, L. (2007). *Tested: One American school struggles to make the grade.* New York, NY: Henry Holt.

Ronda, B. A. (1999). *Elizabeth Palmer Peabody: A reformer on her own terms.* Cambridge, MA: Harvard University Press.

Thoreau, H. D. (2002). *The essays of Henry D. Thoreau*, L. Hyde (Ed.). New York: North Point Press.

CHAPTER 2

RALPH WALDO EMERSON: AWAKENING THE SOUL

"Education is drawing out the Soul"

The work of Ralph Waldo Emerson continues to resonate today. The African American scholar, Charles Johnson (2003), in his introduction to Emerson's writings writes:

> His catholicity—as a standard and challenge—inspires even today, as does his devotion to Reason, which placed him, happily, on the right side of history as a spirited nonconformist, who championed the right of women to vote; who passionately spoke out against slavery in such addresses as "Emancipation in the British West Indies," against the evil of the Fugitive Slave Act, which turned "all the Citizens of this hemisphere into kidnappers," against the "wicked Indian policy"; and who wrestled with the received idea, so common at the time, of the supposed inferiority of blacks. (p. x)

Thomas Moore (2002), who through his extensive writings has restored the word "soul" to the contemporary context, writes that Emerson "represents the best in the spiritual explorer. I cannot read enough by him or about him." (p. 74)

And most relevant to this discussion Harry Lewis, former Dean of Harvard College in his book *Excellence without Soul: Does Liberal Education Have a*

Trancendental Learning: The Educational Legacy of Alcott, Emerson,
Fuller, Peabody and Thoreau, pp. 15–28
Copyright © 2011 by Information Age Publishing
All rights of reproduction in any form reserved.

Future describes how in the 1990s all incoming freshman had to read Emerson's essay "Self-Reliance" and discuss it in small groups.

> Why did Harvard make freshmen read an essay on self-reliance at the moment when it was trying to create community out of diversity? Because the way to free students from the presumptions with which they arrive is to have them believe in themselves as individuals, and not see themselves first as members of identity groups. Self-understanding and confidence in one's principles and judgments are key tools of educated citizens and leaders. (p. 267)

Lewis writes "Harvard teaches students but does not make them wise" (p. 255). He saw the exercise of reading Emerson as an initial effort to bring some wisdom to their first year at Harvard.

This chapter looks at Emerson's vision of education and teaching.

Emerson was the intellectual leader of the Transcendentalists; his small book, *Nature*, published in 1836 inspired Alcott, Fuller, Thoreau and many others at the time. It was a call for each person to have "an original relationship with the universe." He was also mentor to Alcott, Fuller, and Thoreau. Unlike Alcott, Fuller, and Thoreau, who saw themselves as teachers at least for part of their careers, Emerson never enjoyed teaching school; Rusk in his biography of Emerson has a chapter entitled "The Unwilling Schoolmaster." However, he devoted his life to writing and lecturing. He gave 1500 lectures over four decades and saw his lectures as the vehicle for awakening the individual. His writing and lecturing were designed to awaken the soul or what he called the "infinitude" within each person. Emerson saw himself as a Teacher in the larger sense. He wrote: "Teaching is the perpetual end and office of all things. Teaching instruction is the main design that shines through the sky and earth" (Richardson, p. 153).

EARLY INFLUENCES

Emerson was born in Boston in 1803 and lived in Massachusetts his whole life. His father died when he was only eight and was raised by his mother. He had four brothers, who were close growing up. One of the earliest and long-lasting influences was his aunt, Mary Moody Emerson, who read widely and corresponded with Emerson throughout her life. She advised the Emerson boys: "Always do what you are afraid to do" (Richardson, p. 25). She was an iconoclast and encouraged Emerson to seek direct experience rather than following the directions of others.

In 1829, he married Ellen Tucker, who died of tuberculosis two years later. Emerson was an ordained Unitarian minister at the time but her death along with his doubts about church doctrines led him to resign his position. He traveled to Europe and when he returned he began his career of writing and lecturing. It was on this trip that he visited the Jardin de Plantes in Paris (see Chapter 1) that had such a profound impact on his thought. It was this experience that led him to see "how much finer things are in composition than alone" (Richardson, p. 141). Emerson saw the universe as cosmos, or as an ordered, interconnected unity. On this trip, he also met Thomas Carlyle, who became a life-long friend. Carlyle also shared the view that "nothing is separate" (Richardson, p. 174).

Plato was one of the strongest influences on Emerson whose work he felt "invokes the idea of the divine unity" (Richardson, p. 66). Emerson's interest in Plato, however, was balanced by reading Montaigne, whom Emerson saw, a middle ground between Plato's idealism and the realism of Hume.

Coleridge, also a Platonist, was another important influence on Emerson just as he was for Alcott. Coleridge's distinction between Reason, a higher form of intuition, and Understanding, which relies entirely on the senses was important to Emerson's understanding of the mind. Emerson believed that within the mind were the same laws the governed the universe. He (1982) wrote in his journal:

> As long as the soul seeks an external God, it never can have peace, it always must be uncertain.... But when it sees the Great God far within its own nature, then it sees that always itself is party to all that can be, that always it will be informed of that which will happen and there it is pervaded with great peace ... (pp. 151–152)

Viriginia Wolf (1977) said this of Emerson: "What he did was to assert that he could not be rejected because he held the universe within him. Each man, by finding out what he feels, discovers the laws of the universe" (p. 69).

Emerson was deeply influenced by Eastern thought including Hinduism through the *Bhagavad Gita*, Buddhism, and Sufism. He wrote (1982) this about Hinduism in his journals:

> The Indian teaching through its cloud of legends, has yet a simple and grand religion, like a queenly countenance seen through a rich veil. It teaches to speak the truth, love others as yourself, and to despise trifles. The East is grand—and makes Europe appear the land of trifles. Identity, identity! friend and foe are of one stuff, and the stuff is such and so much that the variations of surface are unimportant. All is for the soul, and the soul is Vishnu; and animals and stars are transient paintings; and light is whitewash; and durations are deceptive; and form is imprisonment and heaven itself a decoy. That which the soul seeks is resolution into Being above form ... liberation from existence is its name. Cheerful and noble is the genius of this cosmogony. (pp. 348–349)

Like Fuller, Emerson was drawn to the work of Goethe. One idea that particularly resonated was his concept of *Bildung* or self-cultivation. For both Goethe and Emerson one of the goals of life was self-development and expression and Emerson developed this concept in the essay on Self-Reliance. He (2003) wrote: "Nothing is at last sacred but the integrity of your own mind.... Trust thyself: every heart vibrates to that iron string. Accept the place the divine providence has found for you, the society of your contemporaries, the connection of events" (pp. 268–269).

Emerson's emphasis on the "infinitude" within each person has sometimes been mistaken for egoism. Yet, he and the other Transcendentalists always saw the person as deeply connected to community, the earth and the universe. Although he focused on the dignity and innate wisdom of the soul, this soul is always in a state of relation. We can also look at each of the individuals in this book and how they lived their lives. They certainly were not egotistical individuals but cared for each other, their families and communities. Emerson was loved by his neighbors in Concord and they rebuilt his home after it burned. Margaret Fuller looked after her siblings in a manner that her brother termed "heroic." (see Chapter 4, "Youth")

Nature

As mentioned at the beginning of this chapter, *Nature* was the seminal text of Transcendentalism. At the beginning of the book, Emerson claims that there are two fundamental elements—Nature and Soul. The beauty of nature is the external representation of the beauty of the soul. Emerson (2003) writes:

> In the tranquil landscape, and especially in the distant line of the horizon, man beholds somewhat as beautiful as his own nature.
>
> The greatest delight which the fields and woods minister, is the suggestion of an occult relation between man and the vegetable. I am not alone and unacknowledged. They nod to me, and I to them ...
>
> Yet, it is certain that the power to produce this delight does not reside in nature, but in man, or in a harmony of both. (p.185)

Holism pervades Emerson's view of the universe; each part is a reflection of the whole. "A leaf, a drop, a crystal, a moment of time is related to the whole and partakes of the perfection of the whole. Each particle is a microcosm, and faithfully renders the likeness of the world"(p. 204). Emerson used the circle to represent wholeness as he sees reality as a set of concentric circles. This is an ancient view of reality that indigenous cultures also articulated. Cajete (1994) writes about concentric circles in his book on indigenous education.

> The concentric ring is also a basic symbol of wholeness. It allows for representation of wholeness as the interconnection of many concentric rings of relationship. The mapping of concentric rings of relationship is a major activity

that occurs in primal people's mythology, ritual, and adaptation to their respective natural environments. (p. 119)

Just as Emerson (2003) saw how the human being and world are deeply interconnected, he also saw how everything was changing. "Who looks upon a river in a meditative hour, and is not reminded of the flux of all things.... Nature is not fixed but fluid" (p. 194, 224). For Emerson everything including the soul was in process.

Emerson saw that human beings were becoming alienated from nature. He wrote (2003): "As we degenerate, the contrast between us and our house is more evident. We are as much strangers in nature as we are aliens from God. We do not understand the notes of birds ... We do not know the uses of more than a few plants" (p. 217). What would he say today with climate change and oil spills?

For Emerson, the remedy is the awakening of the soul. He writes: The problem of restoring to the world original and eternal beauty is solved by the redemption of the soul" (p. 222). He was not talking about redemption in the traditional Christian sense but instead seeing "the miraculous in the common" (p. 223). For Emerson that "days are gods" and seeing the world with loving eyes is the beginning of redemption.

CONCORD

In 1835, Emerson married Lydia Jackson and moved to Concord where he lived the rest of his life. He called his wife Lydian and together they had four children, although the first born, Waldo, died tragically at the age of five. His home was destination for many of the Transcendentalists including Margaret Fuller, Alcott, Thoreau and many others. Thoreau sometimes stayed in the home and helped with the children when Emerson was away on his lecture tours. Emerson helped Alcott financially and read through his writings with the hope of reworking of them so they would be readable. He bought the land where Thoreau built his cabin at Walden. Emerson was active in community affairs in Concord and was a life-long member of the school committee. Although he shied away from politics, he became active in the antislavery movement during the 1850s. Emerson was beloved by the Concord community. In 1872, most of his house was ruined by fire although most of his books and papers were saved. He traveled then to Europe and Egypt and when he returned the house had been rebuilt with donations from people living in Concord and Boston. It still stands today and is open to visitors.

In 1837 and 1838, Emerson gave two important addresses that resonated in different ways with his audiences. In 1837, he gave The American Scholar address to the Phi Beta Kappa society at Harvard. It was a call to

American thinkers to forge their own path without reference to European thought. Richardson (1995) argues that the address is "perennially fresh because what is being liberated here is not America—not American literature or the American intelligentsia—but the single person" (p. 265). In this address, Emerson continues with some of the same themes addressed in *Nature*. There is an emphasis on soul when he (2003) says, "The one thing in the world, of value, is the active soul" (p. 230). He continues to see nature in relationship to soul. "In yourself is the law of all nature … it is to you to know all, to dare all" (p. 244). He calls on universities "not to drill but create" and thus "set the hearts of their youth on flame" (p. 232). We could question today, as Harry Lewis (2006), former Dean of Harvard College, how successfully universities have addressed this admonition.

In 1838, he gave an address at the Harvard Divinity School. This address met with a much harsher reaction as he questioned the tenets of traditional Christianity. He began the address by arguing that within each person is a "religious sentiment" which exists within the soul. It seeks beauty, truth, and love. This sentiment is the divine in the human being and problems arise when institutions such as the church deny this sentiment and instead focus on external authority. Emerson (2003) felt that we must find the Christ within rather than look to the doctrines and rituals of the church. "Dare to love God without mediator or veil" (p. 261). Emerson's talk was met with anger and he was not invited to speak at Harvard for several decades. The talk was also attacked in Boston newspapers and Emerson felt the sting of the censure. Because of this rebuke, Richardson argues that his focus on the individual with less emphasis on community is witnessed in the essay on "Self-Reliance" which followed his Divinity School address.

ESSAYS

The 1840s was a period of reformist ideas and communal experiments. Emerson was invited to participate in some of these experiments such as Brook Farm and Fruitlands but he did not participate. He felt participation in the life of Concord met the need for community. In the first half of the 1840s Emerson published two books of essays. A few of the most well known of these include "Self-Reliance," "The Over-Soul," "Circles," and "The Poet."

Self-Reliance

Emerson (2003) continually calls on us to trust ourselves. "Insist on yourself, never imitate." (p. 268) "Nothing is sacred except the integrity of your own mind." (p. 269). He reveres solitude. "It is easy in the world to live after the world's opinions; it is easy in solitude to live after our own" (p. 271). Emerson's walks in the woods surrounding Concord provided this solitude and had a contemplative quality. After these walks, he would go to his study and write down his thoughts in his journal. By the end of his life his journals and note taking totalled 230 volumes.

In solitude, the "mind is simple" and receives divine wisdom. Emerson's "simple mind" is echoed in Suzuki's (1970) "beginner's mind," that is, a mind which is not cluttered with models and concepts but sees clearly. It is empty and through this emptiness wisdom can arise. He calls the wisdom that arises in this way "Intuition." This is a place where "analysis cannot go" and comes from a place where "all life and being" proceed (p. 277). This is the soul.

The Oversoul

At the beginning of this essay Emerson (2003) writes, "Meantime within man is the soul of the whole; the wise silence; the universal beauty, to which every part and particle is equally related; the eternal One" (p. 295). It is the soul which animates the body and intellect. Language is not always the best vehicle for expressing soul as "The action of the soul is oftener in that which is felt and left unsaid than in that which is said in any conversation" (p. 300). This idea has implications for teaching and instructors. "Do not say things. What you are stand over you the while and thunders so that I cannot hear what you say to the contrary" (p. 73).

Emerson claims that if the person has found their center then divinity will shine through that individual. He calls on teachers to speak from *within* or from one's own direct experience. The teacher who can do this inspires the soul of the student. "The great poet makes us feel our own wealth, and then we think less of his compositions." (p. 306) This requires a certain humility as he asks us to "rest in perfect humility" and "to burn with love." I will say more about the Transcendental Teacher in the last two chapters but Emerson offers us a blueprint. He ends this essay with what we might call the "outcome" of teaching with soul.

> Thus revering the soul, and learning, as the ancient said, that "its beauty is immense," man will come to see that the world is the perennial miracle which the soul worketh, and be less astonished at particular wonders; he will learn that there is no profane history; that all history is sacred; that the universe is represented in an atom, in a moment of time. He will live no longer a spotted life of shreds and patches, but he will with a divine unity. (p. 311)

Circles

Emerson saw spiritual growth as ever expanding circles, "The life of man is a self-evolving circle, which, from a ring imperceptibly small, rushes on all sides outwards to new and larger circles and that without end." (p. 314). The degree of expansion depends on the soul. Again for Emerson everything is in transition including the soul. "Nothing is secure but life, transition, the energizing spirit ... Life is a series of surprises" (p. 323). We need to approach life in an open, inquiring manner. Emerson says that he "simply experiments" and is "an endless seeker with no Past" (p. 322). Enthusiasm is important in this quest. "The way of life is wonderful, it is by abandonment" (p. 324).

Emerson's continued emphasis on transition, flux, and change can be traced to his interest in the work of the pre-Socratic philosophers, particularly Thales and Heraclitus. He noted how Thales saw "water was the beginning of all things and how the essence of the soul is motion" (Richardson, p. 104). Richardson (1995) notes that "Heraclitus holds out the possibility of believing in perpetual change and in fixed laws at the same time" (p. 104). The teachings of the Buddha with his emphasis on impermanence may have also influenced Emerson.

The Poet

For Emerson (2003), the poet was the complete person. "He is a beholder of ideas, and utterer of the necessary and casual." These ideas are "so passionate and alive, that, like the spirit of a plant or an animal, it has an architecture of its own, and adorns nature with a new thing" (p. 329). The poet can bring us to a "holy place," and we "should go very warily and reverently" (p. 330). Poets are not confined to a special group, but include anyone who can come in direct contact with nature—"hunters, farmers, grooms and butchers, thought they express their affection in their choice of life, and not in their choice of words." These people love the "earnest of the north wind, or rain, of stone and wood and iron" (p. 333).

The poet sees things holistically as he or she "reattaches things to nature and the Whole" (p. 335). This seeing is not just an intellectual act but as the ancients expressed comes through "the intellect inebriated by nectar" (p. 340). Some try to find this nectar through narcotics but Emerson believes that air, water, and sun should suffice for inspiration. Nature again is the ultimate source. The poet is "free and they make free" (p. 343). They are source of liberation by their ability to share a new thought or symbol.

Emerson wrote the Poet after the death of his child, Waldo. Richardson (1995) believes his writing was source of healing and cites Lewis Mumford, who remarked that Emerson's work is better than Marcus Aurelius' because of "his sense of life's capacity for self-renewal" (p. 375).

EMERSON AND EDUCATON

Emerson wrote two essays on education—"Culture" and "Education" and made several reflections on education in his journals. He was critical of the current approaches to education at his time. He (1966) wrote:

> Whilst we all know in our own experience and apply natural methods in our own business, in education our common sense fails us, and we are continually trying costly machinery against nature, in patent schools and academies and in great colleges and universities. (p. 220)

He also saw how education focused on making people accountants or attorneys rather than "great hearted" human beings (p. 211). This critique could still be applied today as schools and colleges have become training grounds so students can "compete in the global economy." In his journal, he (1982) wrote that "because our education is defective, because we are superficial and ill read, we are forced to make the most of that position of ignorance; to idealize ignorance. Hence America is a vast Know-Nothing Party, and we disparage books" (p. 475).

In contrast, Emerson (1966) offers a different vision of education. Some of his goals for education include:

(1) Self-trust

> The great object of Education should be commensurate with the object of life. It should be a moral one; to teach self-trust, to inspire the youthful man with an interest in himself; with a curiosity touching his own nature; to acquaint him with the resources of his mind to teach that here is all his strength, and to inflame him with a piety towards the Grand Mind in which he lives (p. 211).

(2) Another goal is the development of *imagination and awakening of the soul*, which is connected with what Emerson refers to as the "Vast." He felt that education was spiritual in nature. He (1982) writes in his journal that "Education is drawing out the Soul" (p. 80). Like Bronson Alcott, Emerson believed there was much wisdom within the child that needed to be nurtured and developed. His lectures were designed to stir the souls in his audience. York and Spaulding (2008) write:

> Emerson held one goal for himself as lecturer; to inspire the individual that come to hear him and awaken them to their own potential, to their origin in spirit and the wisdom in nature presented to them every day as picture of the human being in its divine proportion. He sought to be a teacher of the spirit

to his country men, to speak with such force to "get the soul out of bed, out of her deep habitual sleep, out in to God's universe, to a perception of its beauty and hearing of its call, and your vulgar man, your prosy, selfish sensualist awakes, a god, and is conscious of force to shake the world. (p. viii)

This awakening of the soul is continuous theme in Emerson's view of education.

(3) Another goal is to see "all facts in their connection" (1966, p. 205). Emerson's experience at the Jardin des Plantes helped him see the world as interconnected and whole. He (2003) wrote: "Nothing is quite beautiful alone; nothing but is beautiful in the whole. A single object is only so far beautiful as it suggests this universal grace" (p. 192). Education should assist the student in seeing how facts are connected. Instead, our education system has tended to be fragmented with courses, units, lessons, and bits of information with little effort to relate these courses or units to each other so there is little chance to witness the grace that Emerson refers to.

(4) There is also the practical goal in Emerson's vision as he calls for *accuracy*. So, though he wants the children to pursue their interests, they should do it in a careful manner. There is a place for step-by-step learning which helps lead to an "unfolding of thought" and "fullness of power."

Emerson says little about how to achieve these aims. He does advocate an active education where children are outdoors engaged in various games and activities such as camping. These activities should connect with work that is done in school as he encourages the reading of novels, and most of all, poetry. School also offers the opportunity for collegiality and encourages the "practice of conversation, namely to hear as well as to speak" (1966, p. 215). Yet, Emerson also calls for solitude as "the most genial and amiable of men must alternate society with solitude, and learn its severe lessons" (p. 216).

Emerson (1966) says to the teacher "Respect the child" (p. 217). However, he doubts this can be done in the large classroom with many students since the teacher will "grow departmental, routinary, military almost with your discipline" (p. 221). Generally, Emerson opposed too much design. He writes in his essay "Experience" that "Nature hates calculators" and that 'for practical success there must not be too much design" (p. 364). So teachers must ultimately rely on their intuition rather than a rigid curriculum. Instead of discussing curriculum or teaching methods, Emerson focuses on the teacher. In his essay, Emerson (1966) asks teachers to use "the methods of love" (p. 224). One of these methods is patience.

Now the correction of this quack practice is to import into Education the wisdom of life. Leave this military hurry and adopt the pace of Nature. Her secret is patience.... Can you not baffle the impatience and passion of the child by your tranquility? Can you not wait for him, as Nature and Providence do? ... (pp. 224–225)

Emerson (1966) writes that children have secrets and wonderful methods within them. He encourages the teacher to employ sympathy and humor.

> Sympathy, the female force, ... is more subtle and lasting and creative. I advise teachers to cherish mother-wit. I assume that you will keep the grammar, reading, writing and arithmetic in order; 'tis easy and of course you will. But smuggle in a little contraband wit, fancy, imagination, thought. (p. 226)

The presence of the teacher is crucial for Emerson. "That which we are, we shall teach, not voluntarily, but involuntarily" (2003, p. 305). In speaking to teachers he (1966) wrote: "By simple living, by an illimitable soul, you inspire, you correct, you instruct, you raise, you embellish all. By your own act you teacher the behold how to do the practicable. According to the depth from which you draw your life, such is the depth not only of your strenuous effort, but of *your manners and presence* (my italics)" (p. 227).

His comments about a preacher, I believe, also apply to teachers when he writes:

> He had lived in vain. He had not one word intimating that he had laughed or wept, was married or in love, had been commended, or cheated or chagrined. If he had ever lived and acted, we were none the wiser for it. The capital secret of his profession, namely, to convert life into truth, he had not learned. Not one fact in all his experience had he yet imported in to his doctrine. (2003, p. 257)

Students want to know something about their teachers. Frank McCourt (2005) in his book, *Teacher Man*, describes how he told students stories about growing up in Ireland. It was through these stories that he was able to connect with students his first year of teaching high school. He believed these stories allowed him to survive his first year of teaching. He wrote that "his life saved his life."

For Emerson education is ultimately about the soul-to-soul connection between teacher and student. He (2003) wrote "The spirit only can teach ... The man on whom the soul descends, through whom the soul speaks, alone can teach. Courage, piety, love, wisdom, can teach; and every man can open his door to these angels, and they shall bring him the gift of tongues" (p. 255). Much of this connection is nonverbal. "The action of the soul is oftener in that which is felt and left unsaid, than in that which is said in any conversation" (p. 300).

Today, there are educators such as Kessler (2000), Palmer (1998), and myself (2000) who have expanded on the themes that Emerson identifies. Each of these individuals discuss how soul can be brought into education. Kessler defines soul as "the inner life; the depth dimension of human experience; the student's longings for something more than an ordinary, material and fragmented existence" (p. x). Kessler explains how being aware of soul can make a difference in classrooms:

> When soul is present in education, attention shifts. As the quality of attention shifts, we listen with great care not only to what people say but to the messages between the words—tones, gestures, the flicker of feeling across the face. And then we concentrate on what has heart and meaning. The yearning, wonder, wisdom, and confusion of students become central to the curriculum. Questions become as important as answers.
>
>   When soul enters the classroom, masks drop away.... Seeing deeply into the perspective of others, accepting what has felt unworthy in themselves, students discover compassion and begin to learn about forgiveness. (p. x)

In my book *Education and the Soul* I define soul as "a deep and vital energy that gives meaning and direction to our lives"(Miller, 2000, p. 9). Some important aspects of soul include finding meaningful work, seeking love in various forms, acknowledging the dark night of the soul, and learning through contemplation. I also describe how curriculum for the inner life (e.g., journaling, autobiography, imagery work, dream work, and meditation) and connecting with earth can nourish the student's soul.

Palmer (1998) focuses mostly on developing the inner life, or soul of the teacher. He calls on teachers to live the undivided life. "To live divided no more is to find a center for one's life, a center external to the institution and its demands.... One finds solid ground on which to stand outside the institution—the ground of one's own being—and from that ground is better able to resist the deformations that occur when organization values become the landscape of one's inner life" (pp. 167–168). Palmer's call for the undivided life echoes Emerson's self-reliance. His recommendations for nourishing the inner life also echo Emerson's when he writes, "How does one attend to the voice of the teacher within? I have no particular methods to suggest, other than the familiar ones: solitude and silence, meditative reading and walking in the woods, keeping journal, finding a friend who will listen" (pp. 31–32).

The Teacher as Poet

Emerson (2003) saw teaching as an art. Like the poet, teachers can see clearly beyond mere appearances. They are able to connect facts and events to the larger context or the Whole. The poet/teacher

> is caught up in the life of the Universe, his speech is thunder, his thought is law and his words are universally intelligible as the plants and animals. The poet know that he speaks adequately then, only when he speaks somewhat wildly, or, "with the flower of the mind"; not with the intellect used as an

organ, but with the intellect released from all service and suffered to take its direction from its celestial life. (pp. 339–340)

Ultimately, teaching is a spiritual act and Emerson recognized that when he wrote "only the spirit can teach." Teachers as poets are deeply in touch with their own genius, or soul, and this inner connection allows them to connect with the genius of the child. Sardello (1992) comments about learning from the soul:

> Soul learning does not consist of the internalization of knowledge, the determination of right meaning, the achievement of accuracy, but is to be found in what sounds right. That the soul sings was understood by the ancient psychology of the soul of the world—the singing of soul was known as the music of the spheres. (p. 63)

One of the buzz words in education today is outcome. I believe that an Emersonian approach to education would lead to students with "singing souls." I find this a very appealing "outcome" for education.

REFERENCES

Cajete, G. (1994). *Look to the mountain: An ecology of indigenous education.* Durango, CO: Kivaki Press.

Emerson, R. W. (1966). *Emerson on education.* Jones, H. M. (Ed.). New York, NY: Teachers College Press.

Emerson, R. W. (1982). *Emerson in his journals.* J. Porte (Ed.). Cambridge, MA: Harvard University Press.

Emerson, R. W. (2003). *Selected writings of Ralph Waldo Emerson.* New York, NY: Signet.

Johnson, C. (2003). "Introduction" in *Selected writings of Ralph Waldo Emerson* (vii–xvi). New York: Signet.

Kessler, R. (2000). *The soul of education: Helping students find connection, compassion and character at school.* Alexandria, VA: Association for Supervision and Curriculum Development.

Lewis, H. R. (2006). *Excellence without a soul: Does liberal education have a future?* New York, NY: Public Affairs Press.

McCourt, F. (2005). *Teacher man.* New York, NY: Scribner.

Miller, J. P. (2000). *Education and the soul: Toward a spiritual curriculum.* Albany, NY: SUNY press.

Moore, T. (2002). *The soul's religion: Cultivating a profoundly spiritual way of life.* New York, NY: Harper Collins.

Palmer, P. J. (1998). *The courage to teach: Exploring the inner landscape of the teacher's life.* San Francisco, CA: Jossey-Bass.

Richardson, R. D. (1995). *Emerson: The mind on fire.* Berkeley, CA: University of California Press.

Sardello, R. (1992). *Love and the soul: Creating a future for earth*. New York, NY: Harper Collins.

Suzuki, S. (1970). *Zen mind, beginner's mind: Informal talks on Zen meditation and practice*. New York, NY: Weatherhill.

Wolf, V. (1977). Emerson journals in *Books and Portraits*. London: Hogarth Press.

York, M., & Spaulding, R. (2008). "Preface" In R. W. Emerson (Ed.), *Natural history of the intellect* (i–xix). Chicago, IL: Wrightwood Press.

CHAPTER 3

BRONSON ALCOTT: PIONEER IN SPIRITUAL EDUCATION

"To teach, with reference to Eternity"

Among Transcendentalists, Bronson Alcott and Elizabeth Peabody were the most devoted to education and nourishing children's spirituality in that context. Bronson Alcott believed that education was the highest calling and devoted most of his life to different forms of teaching. As a young man, he began schools in Philadelphia and Boston. He was also intensely interested in the development of his own children and, like Piaget, kept extensive notes on their growth and behavior. These records totaled thousands of pages. As a mature man, he began giving "conversations" which were forums for adult learning and these were so popular that he was invited to give them in Ohio and Missouri. In his later years, he was appointed Superintendent of Schools in Concord. Finally, towards the end of his life he started the Concord School of Philosophy. With all these achievements there were almost as many failures. The Temple School in Boston had to be closed due the outrage in Boston over the some of topics for discussions in the school. His commune experiment at Fruitlands was a disaster that led to his withdrawal and depression.

The first part of this chapter describes Alcott's work as an educator with an emphasis on the Temple School and the second part discusses how his ideas are relevant to today's educators working in the field of spirituality in education.

Trancendental Learning: The Educational Legacy of Alcott, Emerson, Fuller, Peabody and Thoreau, pp. 29–43
Copyright © 2011 by Information Age Publishing

ALCOTT'S EARLY CAREER

John Matteson (2007) in his Pulitzer Prize winning biography of Bronson Alcott and his daughter Louisa May describes Alcott's journey with compassion. The journey begins in Connecticut where he was born in 1799. As a boy he loved to play outdoors and recalled that "Nature was my parent and from her.... I learned divine wisdom, even when a child" (p. 17). As a young boy, he and his friends witnessed a total solar eclipse in 1806 and he was so excited that he fell and injured his shoulder while throwing stones at the sun. Almost sixty years later, he was to recall the incident in metaphoric manner that characterized his life as "tilting at the sun but always catching the fall.... I suppose I am to toy with the sunbeams as long as I am dazzled by them" (p. 15). Alcott did not take to the formal lessons offered in school; yet he loved to read and was always on the lookout for books to read from the library or neighbors. One book that continued to influence him throughout his life was *Pilgrim's Progress*. *Pilgrim's Progress* is a moral tale that warns the reader not to the follow the seductive path of acquiring wealth or seeking success; instead, one should focus on the spiritual path. Although Alcott accepts this larger message he does not hold to Christian doctrines espoused in *Pilgrim's Progress*. Jesus' teachings were worthy of being followed but Bronson did not accept him as the Son of God. Like Emerson and Thoreau, he was more ecumenical and believed that Hinduism and Confucianism were also valuable sources of spiritual wisdom. Like most Transcendentalists his own intuitive mind was the final reference point rather than the teachings of others. Matteson (2007) comments "his criterion for an idea was neither whether it was practical or probable, but whether it resonated with his spirit" (p. 22).

Alcott's first teaching job was in 1823, when began his work at school in the town of Cheshire, Connecticut. He was convinced that teaching was the most important vocation a person could choose. He was influenced by the work of the Swiss educator, Johann Pestalozzi, who believed in the inherent goodness of the child. In a contribution to a biography of Pestalozz, I, de Guimps (1889) identifies some of key principles of his pedagogy which Alcott adopted.

- Intuition is the basis of instruction.
- In every branch, teaching should begin with the simplest elements and proceed gradually according to the development of the child, that is, in psychologically connected order.
- The time for learning is not the time for judgment and criticism.
- Teaching should aim at development and not dogmatic exposition.
- The educator should respect the individuality of the pupil.
- The relations between the master and the pupil, especially as to discipline, should be based upon and ruled by love. (p. 108).

The last point is very important, as both Pestalozzi and Alcott believed that the classroom should model itself on the loving family. In his first classroom, Alcott brought flowers to create a warm atmosphere. He built individual desks for the students rather than use the long tables and hard benches that were there. Alcott rejected corporal punishment and established a classroom court where students would discipline each other.

Observations on the Principles and Methods of Infant Instruction

Alcott entered an essay contest sponsored by a Philadelphia paper with an essay entitled *Observations on the Principles and Methods of Infant Instruction.*

He proposed a holistic approach to education as the teaching should address "the whole being of the child." Alcott (1830) argued that there were four major faculties within the child: "the animal nature, the affections, the conscience [and] the intellect." By animal nature Alcott is referring to the physical development of the child, which is extremely important in the very young. Like Rudolf Steiner, Alcott argued that the physical development should be nourished which will provide a foundation for later intellectual growth. Instruction should contain "interest, certainty, and love." (pp. 4–6).

Alcott believed in the use of Socratic dialogue to stimulate the conscience and the intellect. Conversation with the children was fundamental to all of Alcott's teaching. Referring to how Jesus taught, he liked using parables and stories as a way to engage the children.

Alcott's essay did not win the prize but it motivated one of its readers, Reuben Haines, to ask Alcott to open a school in Germantown, Pennsylvania based on the principles described in *Observations*. Shortly after arriving in Germantown Alcott's wife gave birth to their first daughter, Anna. With Anna's arrival, Alcott began taking notes regarding the development of the child, which continued with the next two children. This resulted in a total of 2,500 pages of observations and reflections. The ultimate goal in this process was to nourish the happiness and independence of his children.

Around this time Alcott read *Aids to Reflection* by Samuel Taylor Coleridge. Along with *Pilgrim's Progress*, Coleridge's ideas had a powerful impact on Alcott's thinking. Coleridge argued that human beings have the capacity to directly intuit divine truth through what he called Reason; in contrast, Understanding depended on the senses. Implicit in Coleridge's view was that the spiritual was seen as the primary reality and the physical world an imperfect mirror of this reality. Reading Coleridge changed the focus on Alcott's observations of his children; he now focused more on their spiritual development rather than just recording their behaviors. However, he never developed a stage theory of spiritual development such as James Fowler's.

The school in Germantown got off to a promising start, but the sponsor died and thus there was no more financial support for the Alcotts and the school. The school had to be closed. The Alcott's moved to Philadelphia where he started another school but this too failed, as his unconventional teaching methods seemed to scare off the parents. Alcott was convinced that a school could succeed in Boston and moved there in 1834.

THE TEMPLE SCHOOL

With the help of Elizabeth Peabody, Alcott opened the Temple School in Boston. Elizabeth Peabody (see Chapter 6), who later started the kindergarten movement in the U.S, was instrumental to the opening of the Temple School. Well known in Boston, she had been planning on opening her own school when she met Alcott. He showed her some of the conversations that he had with students in his school in Philadelphia and she was very impressed. She wrote to her sister Mary that Bronson was "like an embodiment of intellectual light" and was "destined ... to make a new era in society" (Marshall, p. 295). Elizabeth knew 10 languages as well as philosophy, history and literature. She agreed to help Bronson in the school by teaching and, most importantly, recording the conversations that Bronson conducted with the children.

The setting for the school was the Masonic Temple on Tremont Street. The building was a center of Boston cultural life with concerts and lectures. The school was on the top two floors and the main classroom was a large spacious room which Peabody and Bronson furnished with plants, paintings and busts of Socrates, Plato, Jesus, and Shakespeare. Special desks were handmade for the students.

Reading was taught by using phonics and word recognition. Bronson asked the students to see the word in their mind's eye. Like Montessori and Ashton Warner, he also encouraged students to begin writing and not to wait till they were proficient in reading. Students were encouraged to express their ideas. Although self-expression was encouraged, there was a structure to the day and unruly behavior was not tolerated. Bronson rarely used corporal punishment, and instead he would remove a student from the classes and have the child sit alone. He experimented with different disciplining procedures and once he asked two students who had misbehaved to hit him because he wanted to demonstrate how painful it is to punish another person.

By the winter the enrollment had doubled. Elizabeth Peabody, who had first contracted to work just 2 hours a day, now stayed for the entire school day and began to keep her record of the school. According to Bedell, (1980), *The Record of a School* remains today probably the best exploration of

Bronson Alcott's theories on education" (p. 102). Published in 1835, the book was part of larger movement of social change that included women's rights and antislavery activities. Bedell suggests that *Record of a School* became a "symbol of a whole new era in American thought" (p. 103). Alcott himself had never been happier or felt more fulfilled. He wrote that he had found "a unity and a fullness" in his existence.

The most unusual feature of the school was the conversations that Bronson held with students regarding spiritual matters. Elizabeth Peabody wrote of the school in the *Record* that "Everything in education depends on the view taken of the soul" (p. 182). Alice Howell (1991) writes how Bronson was able to incorporate this attitude into his teaching:

> That the child is not a *tabula rasa* Alcott proves without a doubt. As we read we rediscover that children are far more capable of philosophical insights and intuitions than we usually think, that indeed they take delight in being taken seriously as individuals whose opinions are worthy of respect.... Alcott's secret, and I believe, his success consisted in his approach to children; he worked from his own innermost center toward the same one he knew existed in each of them. A bond of trust, mutual respect, and affection was established at that level, so that the usual ego-to-ego tussle between teacher and student was avoided. (p. xxxii)

The second year of the school opened with 40 students. It was during the period when the abolition movement in New England was growing so there was sense of unrest. Alcott was now in his 30s and most biographers including Matteson and Bedell suggest that at this age, he tended to become self-absorbed, even narcissistic in his behavior. The conversations at the school began to explore areas that Elizabeth Peabody was uncomfortable with. As noted above, Alcott believed that within every child there was an inner wisdom and this is what he wanted to draw out through the conversations. At the same time, he seemed to have an "agenda" and Peabody found that Bronson would change the wording of what was said to confirm his own view. These conversations were originally published as *Conversations with Children on the Gospels* and today have been published as *How Like An Angel Came I Down*.

Matteson states that this book may have been Bronson's "most exquisite work" (p. 76). However, there were a few passages that led to a very hostile reaction in the Boston community. Peabody asked him to remove the material where one child referred to conception and birth as "naughtiness" but Alcott only moved this material to end of the book.

Alcott would have been wise to have followed Peabody's advice, because when the book was published it was called "radically false" in an editorial in one of the Boston papers; another Boston paper called the book "obscene." Emerson and Fuller defended Alcott, but the damage was done. Enrollment declined, and Alcott had to auction off much of the furniture and books. The school moved downstairs into a smaller room. Enrollment dwindled down to a few students. One of the few remaining students, who had recently enrolled in 1839, was Susan Robinson, who was black. When parents of the remaining students heard this, they sent Alcott an ultimatum: Susan must go or they would withdraw their children. To his great credit, Alcott ignored the ultimatum. After the students were withdrawn there were only five students, including three of his own children. He was forced to close the school but as Matteson states, the end of the school was not "under a cloud of disgrace but in a small significant blaze of courage" (p. 85).

With the closing of the Temple School, one is reminded of the failure of some of the free schools in the 60s and 70s because the leaders of these schools became self-absorbed in their own educational ideologies. Alcott's refusal to listen to Elizabeth Peabody has likewise been attributed to self-absorption. Despite the problems, the Temple School provides many inspiring examples of holistic learning and spirituality in education. These will be discussed in the second half of the chapter.

CONVERSATIONS

In 1848, Bronson began public conversations. Alcott was never a good public speaker, but in a smaller setting he enjoyed engaging the audience in dialogue. Alcott (1872) believed that "Debate is angular, conversation circular and radiant of the underlying unity.... Conversation presupposes a common sympathy in the subject, a great equality in the speakers; absence of egotism, a tender criticism of what is spoken.... Conversation with plain people proves more agreeable and profitable, usually, than with companies more pretentious and critical" (p. 73, 76).

The theme of the conversations would focus on an individual such as Dante and how that person represented a certain ideal. This theme provided the beginning, but Matteson compares Alcott's performance at these conversations to a jazz soloist, as he would shift the focus of the conversation as he listened to the concerns of the audience. Over time Bronson was increasingly asked to do the conversations in different settings. In 1852 , students at Harvard Divinity School asked him to lead discussions on "Modern Life." In the fall of 1853, he was invited to give his conversations in what was then called "the West" which included Syracuse, Rochester, Buffalo, Cincinnati and Cleveland.

During the Civil War, Alcott focused his conversations on people that he knew. For example, he discussed "Nature" with extensive references to Thoreau and a conversation on "Letters" that included a discussion of his friends Emerson and Hawthorne. Alcott was 62 years old now, and Matteson notes that his conversations more and more began to revolve around his life-long friends. The discussion became more personal and concrete and much less abstract than his talks and writing when he was younger. In short, he saw how a person was just as important as an idea; the conversations tended to more biography and narrative than exploring abstract ideas. His conversations received positive reviews in the newspapers. As his daughter, Louisa became famous with the publication of *Little Women* he was often asked to speak about his daughter after he had discussed "Hawthorne the Novelist, Thoreau the Naturalist, and Emerson the Rhapsodist." He now referred to his conversations as "the popular conversation." He wrote "I am introduced as the father of Little Women, and I am riding in the Chariot of Glory where I go" (cited in Matteson, p. 364).

ALCOTT'S CONTRIBUTIONS TO TEACHING AND LEARNING

Bronson Alcott's main contribution to education was in his view of the child. He believed that all children held an inner spiritual core that could be drawn out through questioning. The goal of this work was self-knowledge. In *The Record of the School* Peabody (1845) writes that Alcott " was glad to hear that one of the scholars had said out of school, that it was impossible to remain in Mr. Alcott's school and not learn to know one's self "(p. 85). Since the self was closely connected to the soul, the development of the soul was also a goal. Alcott accepted a Platonic view of the soul that it contained a inner wisdom that needed to be drawn out.

Again Peabody (1845) quotes Alcott:

> We need schools not for the inculcation of knowledge, merely, but the development of genius. Genius is the peculiar attribute of the soul. It is the soul, indeed, in full and harmonious play; and no instruction deserves the name, that does not quicken this its essential life, and fit it for representation in literature, art, or philosophy. (p. 17)

In the last two decades, we have seen educators write about the importance of the soul in education (Kessler, 2000; Miller, 2000). Alcott and the other Transcendentalists developed a nonsectarian language about the soul that is helpful today. Soul is often connected to religion but Alcott and Emerson used the term in a manner that allows for an inclusive approach to spiritual education.

Alcott's teaching methods for holistic learning deserve examination since their ultimate aim is the development of the whole person. These methods include Socratic questioning, journals and autobiography, classroom circles, inquiry, imagery and that elusive quality of presence in teaching.

Socratic Questioning

One element of this blueprint was Socratic questioning to draw out the inner wisdom of the students. Below are examples of his questioning from the Temple School, which took place within Alcott's Transcendental/Christian perspective. Alcott and the other Transcendentalists believed that the Christ spirit existed within each individual. Howell (1991) notes that "Alcott was far more universalist in his outlook—he felt that his method of education (*ex-ducere*-leading forth) transcended all sects" (p. xxii).

Below are excerpts from the conversations with children (ages 5–12) selected by Stephen Mitchell in the forward to *How Like an Angel Came I Down*. Mitchell comments that the students in the Temple School "recognize him as one of those rare adults, perhaps the *only* one, who speaks to them with complete sincerity and respect, not as mere children, but as equals"(xiii).

MR. ALCOTT: *Now, does our spirit differ in any sense from God's spirit? Each may answer.*

CHARLES: *(10–12 years old). God made our spirits.*

MR. ALCOTT: *They differ from His then in being derived?*

GEORGE K: *(7–10). They are not so good.*

WILLIAM B: *(10–12). They have not so much power.*

AUGUSTINE: *(7–10). I don't think our spirit does differ much.*

CHARLES: *God is spirit, we are spirit and body.*

JOSIAH: *(5 years old). He differs from us, as a king's body differs from ours. A king's body is arrayed with more goodness than ours.*

EDWARD B: *(10–12). God's spirit is a million times larger than ours, and we come out of him as the drops of the ocean.*

* * *

MR. ALCOTT: *Jesus said he was the son—the child of God. Are we also God's sons?*

WILLIAM B: *Oh! before I was born—I think I was part of God himself.*

MANY OTHERS: *So do I.*

MR. ALCOTT: *Who thinks his own spirit is the child of God?* (All held up hands). *Now, is God your Father in the same sense that he is the Father of Jesus?* (Most held up hands.)

* * *

MR. ALCOTT: *Do you think that were you to use all that is in your spirit, you might also be prophets?*

SEVERAL: *If we had faith enough.*
WILLIAM B: *If we had love enough.*
CHARLES: *A prophet first has a little love, and that gives the impulse to more, and so on, until he becomes so full of love, he knows everything.*

* * *

ELLEN: (10–12) [mentions *"Judgment Day"*]
MR. ALCOTT: *What do you mean by Judgment Day?*
ELLEN: *The last day, the day when the world is to be destroyed.*
CHARLES: *The day of Judgment is not any more at the end of the world than now. It is the Judgment of conscience at every moment.*

* * *

MR. ALCOTT: *Where did Jesus get his knowledge?*
MARTHA (7–10):   *He went into his own soul.*

* * *

JOSIAH (age 5):   *Mr. Alcott, we think too much about clay. We should think of spirit. I think we should love spirit, not clay. I should think a mother now would love her baby's spirit; and suppose it should die, that is only the spirit bursting away out of the body. It is alive; it is happy. I really do not know why people mourn when their friends die. I think it should be a matter of rejoicing. For instance, now, if we should go into the street and find a box, an old dusty box, and should put into it some very fine pearls. And bye and bye the box should grow old and break, why, we should not even think about the box; but if the pearls were safe, we should think of them and nothing else. So it is with the soul and body. I cannot see why people mourn for bodies.*

* * *

MR. ALCOTT: *Do you think these conversations are of any use to you?*
CHARLES: *Yes, they teach us a great deal.*
MR. ALCOTT: *What do they teach you?*
GEORGE K: *To know ourselves.*

(cited in Alcott, 1991, pp. xiii–xvi)

Alcott held these conversations once a week. He would start with story or passage from the Bible as starting point for the discussions. These examples demonstrate Alcott's belief that wisdom lies within and can be drawn out from the student. Most religious education at time involved indoctrination rather than the kind of questioning that Alcott employed. It is clear that Alcott was able to create a safe learning environment where children could express their thoughts and feelings. In short, he created what David Hay (2006) refers to as compassionate concern and Barbara Myers calls 'hospitable space' (cited in Hay, p. 154).

David Hay has also argued that there is a universal quality to children's spiritual experience, which he calls relational consciousness. He describes four different types of relational consciousness: child–God, child–people, child–world, and child–self. Alcott's conversations support Hay's theory as these different aspects can be seen in the examples above. For example, in the last one George refers to self-knowledge while several of the conversations demonstrate child—God consciousness. There is also a conversation on love that is an example of child—other consciousness.

Both Alcott and Hay show a deep respect for the child's intelligence. Matteson identified the qualities that made Alcott a great teacher—"his patience, his love of trying new methods, and his fascination with the slow mysterious progress of children" (p. 249). These qualities are still relevant today for teachers attempting to nurture children's spiritual development.

Journal Writing

Just as Transcendentalists such as Thoreau and Alcott kept journals, they encouraged their students to do the same. At the Temple School, the first task in the morning was for the students to write in their journals. Peabody (1845) records one morning when Alcott was talking to one student.

> Mr. Alcott, who was walking around as usual, was saying to one of the journalists: You are engaged in recording what happens *out of you*; its advantage is to make you feel and remember what *effect* all outward events, and your action on what is outward, may have on your inward state of mind. You write down the picture made on your mind by things. I hope you will soon write the thoughts and feelings that come from your soul about these things. These thoughts and feelings are your inward life. (p. 25)

Alcott encouraged the students not to just record events but to explore how these events relate to their inner life. Together with the Socratic questioning the journals allowed the children to become aware of their soul life.

Autobiography/Biography

Closely connected to journal writing was narrative and autobiography. In the *Record of a School,* Peabody writes about how Alcott saw autobiography as a way for the more mature student to reflect on the development of the soul (p. 193). Alcott also saw autobiography as a better way to develop writing skills. Peabody (1845) writes about this approach:

> Everyone knows that a technical memory of words, and of rules of composition, gives very little command of language; while a rich consciousness, a quick imagination and force of feeling, seem to unlock the treasury; and even so vulgar passion as anger, produces eloquence, and quickens the perception (p. 193).

This is a holistic approach to acquiring writing skills as Alcott wants to engage the whole student in the process.

Inquiry Based Learning

Alcott rarely lectured to the students but led them through a series of questions. Peabody records many examples in *Record of a School.* Sometimes this would involve extended questioning of one pupil or just presenting a general question to the entire class such as "what is the imagination" (p. 165). Sometimes the questions were very leading so that Peabody once wrote that he "unconsciously led them to his views" (p. 158). Bickman (1999) writes about this same tendency: "Alcott's conduct of the classroom and the discussion was sometimes unconsciously manipulative, but he was also much of the time a good listener and provocative questioner" (p. xxiii).

Classroom Circles

Alcott had the students sit in a semicircle rather than in rows, which was very unusual for that time. The semicircle supported the discussion amongst the students since they could see each other's faces. The use of the circle as a vehicle for meeting and discussion can be traced back to indigenous peoples. For example, some First Nations people form a circle and pass the talking stick around to give each person a chance to share their thoughts and feelings. Black Elk said this about circles:

> Everything the Power of the World does is done in a circle.
>   The sky is round, and I have heard that the earth is round like a ball, and so are all the stars. The wind, in its greatest power, whirls. Birds make their

nests in circles, for theirs is the same religion as ours.... The life (of a person) is a circle from childhood to childhood, and it is in everything where power moves. (Baldwin, 1994, p. 80)

Emerson's (2003) essay on "Circles" confirms their importance in the universe as he wrote "the natural world may be conceived of as a system of concentric circles." (p. 320)

Images/Visualization

Alcott used pictures and images to teach language. Peabody (1845) describes his approach in the *Record of a School*.

> When children are committed to his charge very young the first discipline to which he puts them, is of the eye; by making them familiar with pictures. The art of drawing has been well called the art of learning to see.... It is from considerations of this kind that Mr Alcott very early presents to children pictured forms of things; and he selects them in the confidence that the general character of these forms will do much towards setting the direction of the current activity. (pp. 4–5)

The image can help the student to develop their own inner images which is important in the development of imagination. Steiner and other educators (Gaylean, 1983; Murdock 1982) have argued that elementary school children need to develop their imagination and that stories, fairy tales and myths are helpful in this process because they trigger the inner life of the child.

Alcott believed that learning to read and write was facilitated by having children have direct sense experiences. He felt that sight was particularly important and he showed pictures of words and encouraged the students to draw. Peabody (1845) describes the importance of drawing and writing at a very early age. "To aid the practice of the eye, in looking at forms, the practice of the hand in imitating them should soon follow. Mr Alcott thinks the slate and pencil, or the chalk and black board, can hardly be given too early. The latter is even better than the former; for children should have free scope, as we find that their first shapings are almost gigantic" (p. 5). The idea that writing should proceed, or go hand in hand with reading, has also been advocated by Montessori, Steiner and Asthon-Warner. For example, Ashton-Warner (1964) encouraged Maori children in New Zealand to make pictures of their stories.

The Presence of the Teacher

Like Montessori, Alcott saw the teacher as a guide. Matteson (2007) summarizes the role when he writes, "the role of the teacher was neither to drive nor to lead the child; it was to accompany him" (p. 42). Most of all, teachers make a difference through their presence. Alcott (1830) wrote this in his *Observations*:

> The teachers should unite an amiableness of temper, a simplicity of manner, and devotion to his work, which shall associate with it his happiness and duty.... He should possess the power of reaching the infant understanding in the simplest and happiest forms.... Free from prejudices and particularities, he should impart instructions from the pure fountain of truth and love alone. Taking a benevolent view of the works of nature and the ways of Providence, his piety should diffuse itself through all his teachings. (p. 8)

Today Parker Palmer (1998) and Rachael Kessler (n.d.) have argued for the importance of teacher presence. Palmer emphasizes identity and integrity in the teacher. Kessler wrote "We celebrate those precious moments when we embody a "presence" that carries the class to place a where minds and hearts are moved and genuine connections occur" (p. 1). David Hay (2006) suggests awareness exercises such as eating an apple as ways of enhancing presence. (p. 156). This exercise facilitates being more aware and thus more mindful. Mindfulness is discussed in more detail in the last two chapters. To enhance the teacher's presence Alcott encouraged self-reflection. Peabody (1845), in the last chapter of her book, argues that teachers and parents must also embark on the path of self-knowledge if the students are to know themselves. "The parent or teacher should make it his first business to know himself; for most surely he will transmit his moral character by inspiration to his child in just such proportion as circumstances allow to have any influence, and the child has any sensibility" (p. 187).

Adult Education

With his conversations and the Concord School of Philosophy Alcott focused on adult education toward the end of his life. He realized that adults did not want to be just lectured to but engaged in dialogue and discussion. Along with Margaret Fuller, who held similar conversations with women in Boston, Alcott explored how adults could be engaged in learning through this process.

CONCLUSION

Alcott has left an important educational legacy. Along with the other Transcendentalists, he developed an inspiring vision of education that provides a humane alternative to the narrow economic vision of education today.

We can also learn from Alcott's pedagogy. As I have argued, he was a forerunner of Montessori, Steiner, and Ashton-Warner. Central to his vision was the child's inner spiritual core; Montessori called this core the *spiritual embryo*. Alcott's teaching methods such as Socratic questioning, the use of journals and autobiography, and seating the children in a circle were just some of the tools he experimented with to nourish the embryo. Alcott's pedagogy was not limited to spiritual education as he had many interesting ideas regarding how children learn to read and write. We could also benefit from his willingness to experiment and to try various teaching methods to engage children. Most of all, we need to see children as he did—human beings with a mysterious inner life that should be witnessed and nourished.

REFERENCES

Alcott, A. Bronson. (1830). *Observations on the principles and methods of infant instruction*. Boston: Carter and Hendee.

Alcott, A. Bronson. (1872). *Concord days*. Boston: Robert Brothers.

Alcott, A. B. (1991). *How like an angel came I down: Conversations with children on the Gospels*. A. O. Howell (Ed.). Hudson, NY: Lindisfarne Press.

Ashton-Warner, S. (1964). *Teacher*. New York, NY: Bantam

Baldwin, C. (1994). *Calling the circle: The First and future culture*. Newberg, Oregon: Swan Raven.

Bedell, M. (1980). *The Alcotts: Biography of a family*. New York, NY: Clarkson N. Potter.

Bickman, M. (Ed.). (1999). *Uncommon learning: Henry David Thoreau on education*. Boston: Houghton Mifflin.

de Guimps, R. (1889). *Pestalozzi: His aim and work*. Syracuse, NY: C. W. Bardeen.

Emerson, R. W. (2003). *Selected writings of Ralph Waldo Emerson*. New York, NY: Signet.

Gaylean, B. (1983). *Mindsight: Learning through imaging*. Healdsburg, CA: Center for Integrative Learning.

Hay, D. & R. Nye. (2006). *The spirit of the child*. London; Jessica Kingsley.

Howell, A. O. (1991). "Introduction and the soul of the child" in *How like an angel came I down*. Alcott, A. B. Hudson, NY: Lindisfarne Press, xvii–xliv.

Kessler, R. (2000). *The soul of education: Helping students find connection, compassion, and character at school*. Alexandria, VA: Association for Supervision and Curriculum Development.

Kessler, R. (n.d.). The Teaching presence. Unpublished paper.

Marshall, M. (2005). *The Peabody sisters: Three women who ignited American romanticism*. Boston: Houghton Mifflin.

Matteson, J. (2007). *Eden's outcasts: The story of Louis May Alcott and her Father.* New York, NY: W. W. Norton.

Miller, J. P. (2000). *Education and the soul: Toward a spiritual curriculum*. Albany, NY: SUNY Press.

Murdock, M. (1982). *Spinning inward: Using guided imagery with children*. Culver, CA: Peace Press.

Palmer, P. J. (1998). *The courage to teach: Exploring the inner landscape of a teacher's life*. San Francisco, CA: Jossey-Bass.

Peabody, E. (1845). *Record of a school: Exemplifying the general principles of spiritual culture*. Bedford MA: Applewood Books.

Note: Much of this chapter appeared as an article entitled "Bronson Alcott: Pioneer in Spiritual Education." in the *International Journal of Children's Spirituality*. May, 2010 **15**: 129–142.

CHAPTER 4

MARGARET FULLER: VOICE FOR AND EDUCATOR OF WOMEN

It is therefore that I would have woman lay aside all thought, such as she habitually cherishes of being taught and led by men

In discussing the Transcendentalists in his book on antebellum America, *What has God Wrought*, Daniel Howe (2007) asserts that "From our standpoint in the 21st century, The Transcendentalist who looks most "modern" is Margaret Fuller. Versatile and passionate she made her impact felt on journalism, feminism,, criticism (literary, music, and art,) and revolution" (p. 621). I would add education to that list with her focus on education for women. Fuller believed that women should develop their full potential. In her book *Woman in the Nineteenth Century*, she (1992) wrote, "But if you ask me what offices they may fill: I reply—any. I do not care what case you put; Let them be sea-captains if they will" (p. 345). Von Mehren (1994) argues that she called on women to employ both their intellect and their intuition.

> Her program emphasized the development of intellectual discipline, critical intelligence, and self-awareness—qualities she categorized as Minerva-like powers—as needed balance to woman's already overdeveloped emotional, intuitional, divinatory, or Muse-like qualities. She believed that bringing into

Trancendental Learning: The Educational Legacy of Alcott, Emerson, Fuller, Peabody and Thoreau, pp. 45–58

harmony Minerva and the Muse would endow woman with the power to sub-
due cultural opposition and take her place as man's equal in society (p. 3).

In this chapter, I describe Fuller's activities as an educator and then
explore their implications for teaching and learning. For those seeking a
holistic approach to education she offers important insights particularly
regarding the education of women.

YOUTH

Margaret's father, Timothy Fuller, was the strongest influence in her childhood. Her father was member of the U.S. House of Representatives so was
away for part of the year. When he was home in Cambridgeport, Massachusetts, he would instruct her late into the evening. By age six, he was giving
Margaret lessons in English grammar and Latin. At age 9, she was reading
biographies and political histories as well as major texts of Latin literature.
Her father held a conflicted view of women as he expected his wife to be
passive and follow his directives yet he educated his daughter the way that
men were educated at the time. Capper (2002) in his biography of Margaret writes that her father made clear to his wife that he was "substituting
rational criticism for affection" in teaching his daughter (p. 35). Von
Mehren (1994) concludes that as result of this instruction Margaret "developed a well-stored mind, a remarkable facility with the spoken word and
with foreign languages and the exhilarating sense that she was very alive
under tension" (p. 17).

Later in her life she reflected on her father's influence and felt that over
rationalistic approach was damaging. In her words:

> ….as he was a severe teacher, both from his habits and ambitions for me, my
> feelings were kept on the stretch till the recitations were over. Thus, fre-
> quently, I was sent to bed several hours too late, with nerves unnaturally stim-
> ulated. The consequence was premature development of the brain, that
> made me a "youthful prodigy" by day, and by night a victim of spectral illu-
> sions, night-mares, and somnambulism, which at the time prevented the har-
> monious development of my bodily powers and checked my growth, while,
> later, they induced continual headache, weakness and nervous affections, of
> all kinds…
>
> Trained to great dexterity in artificial methods, accurate, ready, with entire
> command of his resources, he had no belief in minds that listen, wait, and
> receive. He had no conception of the subtle and indirect motions of imagina-
> tion and feeling. His influence on me was great, and opposed to the natural
> unfolding of my character, which was fervent, of strong grasp, and disposed
> to infatuation, and self-forgetfulness. (1992, p. 26, p. 28)

Here, is a capsule vision of Fuller's view of learning and development as she believes in the importance of "natural unfolding" and the importance of "imagination and feelings." When Fuller was traveling on the Great Lakes as a young woman, she met a parent who embodied her vision and she wrote, "He was one of those parents—why so rare?—who understand and live a new life in that of their children, instead of wasting time and young happiness in trying to make them conform to an object and standard of their own. The character and history of each child may be a new and poetic experience to the parent." (p. 219)

Capper (2002) concludes that the father's teaching led to the imposition of a false intellectual self that was alien from her deeper identity (p. 36). Murray speculates that the late night sessions with her father had an erotic, even possibly incestuous element. Whatever happened in those late night sessions Murray believes that left a lasting impact on Margaret in form of what Shengold calls "soul murder." Murray believes that Margaret struggled her whole life to free her inner self from the psychological hold of her father (p. 273). Whatever the case, Margaret, like the other Transcendentalists, believed that education should be a natural unfolding of the soul rather than the imposition of an alien, intellectual self.

Margaret had several younger siblings whom she taught and cared for; her brother, Richard, wrote about her efforts:

> When now, with the experience of a man, I look back upon her wise guardianship over our childhood, her indefatigable labors for our education, her constant supervision in our family affairs, her minute instruction as to the management of multifarious details, her painful conscientiousness in every duty; and then reflect on her native inaptitude and even disgust for practical affairs, on her sacrifice—in the very flower of her genius—of her favorite pursuits, on her incessant drudgery and waste of health, on her patient bearing of burdens, and courageous conflict with difficult circumstances, her character stands before me as heroic. (Fuller, 1860, p. 125)

As an adolescent, she was deeply influenced by Rousseau and his views of education in *Emile* though she would develop a different view of how women should be educated. Still she accepted that the child's nature was basically good and needed to be nourished so that goodness could unfold. She saw the universe as an organic whole and the individual's awareness of that wholeness could be realized through "nonrational perceptions" (Capper, p. 91). The strongest intellectual influence on the young Fuller was Goethe. Capper writes that Goethe's "idea of the progressive evolution of personal character through the natural unfolding of one's inner self, his quasi-paganistic religious views, … even his sensualism were all ideas that found echoes in the kind of naturalistic romanticism that Fuller had been cultivating since her adolescence" (p. 129). She spent many years doing research on a biography of Goethe which never came to fruition.

When she was 21 years, she had a mystical experience sitting by a pool of water.

> I did not think; all was dark, and cold, and still. Suddenly the sun shone out with that transparent sweetness, like the last smile of a dying lover, which it will use when it has been unkind all a cold autumn day. And, even then, passed into my thought a beam from its true sun, from its native sphere, which has never since departed from me. I remember how, a little child, I had stopped myself one day on the stairs, and asked, how came I here? How is it that I seem to be this Margaret Fuller? What does it mean? What shall I do about it? I remembered all the times and ways in which the same thought returned. I saw how long it must be before the soul can learn to act under these limitations of time and space, and human nature; but I saw, also, that it MUST do it—that I must make this false true—and how new and immortal plants in the garden of God, before it could return again. I saw there was no self; that selfishness was all folly, and the result of circumstance; that it was only because I thought self real that I suffered; that I had only to live in the idea of the ALL, and all was mine. This truth came to me, and I receive it unhesitatingly; so that I was for that hour taken up into God. In that true ray of most of the relations of earth seemed mere films, phenomena. (1992, p. 11)

Although she did not have many experiences like this one, she called herself a "mystic." She (1992) wrote in her journal, "Nothing interests me except listening to the secret harmonies of nature" (p. 12).

TEACHING SCHOOL

When Margaret was 26, she went to the annual meeting of the American Institute of Instruction at Worcester and Von Mehren states that this "marked her decision to enter teaching professionally" (p. 80). The main speaker at the meeting was Bronson Alcott and her acquaintance with him led to her involvement in the Temple School (see Chapter 3). After Elizabeth Peabody resigned because of her disagreements with Alcott, Margaret taught Latin, French and Italian and kept records of Alcott's conversations with the students. However, the school soon closed over controversy that arose from the publication of *Conversation on the Gospels*.

After the closing of the Temple School, Margaret moved to Providence to teach at the Greene Street School for girls. She found herself in charge of 60 of the 150 students and taught "Latin, composition, elocution, history, natural philosophy and ethics." A few years before she had met Emerson whose work inspired her and she wrote him about her philosophy of education that included "Activity of mind, accuracy in processes, and ... search after the good and beautiful" (Capper, p. 212). Her teaching seemed to resonate better with the older girls with her intellectually challenging methods. Her discipline was strict but once the students protested her treatment of one student causing Margaret to apologize for being "too rough". She wrote to the students:

> ... let me take this opportunity to say that it is not because I do not value you and even (I use no the word lightly) love you. If I did not wish to *give* my love, some of my scholars would *gain* it by their uniformly honorable conduct and engaging manners. And you will do me justice in believing that I generally feel much more regard than I express. And, though I cannot do for you all that another might in my place, let me assure you that, if, while under my care of after you leave me, you should feel that I can, by any counsel or words of instruction or act of kindness, benefit you where others could, not my ear and heart will always be ready to attend to your wishes. (Myerson, 2008, p. 15)

Many of the students expressed strong affection for her and one student wrote:

> I cannot find words to express my love for dear Miss Fuller, you who know her so well can better conceive it than I describe. She is everything to me, my teacher, my counselor, my guide, my friend, my pillar on which I lean for support when disheartened and discourage, and she allows me to look upon her as such.... I had no idea she had so much heart, but it is overflowing with affection and love. (Myerson, p. 16)

She also challenged her students to think for themselves and as she would do later in Boston with women she engaged in conversations. Although she consistently impressed the students with her knowledge, she always left time for students to engage the material themselves through discussion. One student said, "We must talk and let her understand our minds" (Capper, p. 232). She had the students keep journals so there is record of students' reactions to her teaching. She also asked the students to avoid "stiff and formal" expression to write more freely.

Margaret taught a course in ethics where she introduced some Transcendental ideas to her students such as the inherent goodness and beauty of the soul. But she also did not hesitate to lecture the students about the importance of female culture by reading female authors and studying the achievements of women in history. She also told myths that involved women such as the wild huntress Atlanta and Daphne. Capper speculates on the impact of Fuller's teaching on the students. She cites one student who wrote that she and others in her class did not "live to dress and visit, and gossip and get married. They are studious to improve themselves, to do good, and live for their higher natures" (p. 236).

Fuller found the teaching stressful and she suffered from headaches. She ended her term at the school in December, 1838. One of her students, Mary Ware Allen, describes that last meeting and how Margaret spoke of the importance of her "religion."

> ... she said her whole aim had been to inspire us with a love and respect for religion, to look upon it as the only thing which we could lean for consolation and peace here and for happiness here-after. (Myerson, p. 18)

Margaret spoke of the last meeting and used the word "spiritual" instead of religion as the basic aim of her teaching:

> I assured them of my true friendship, proved by my never having cajoled or caressed them into good. Every word of praise had been earned; all my influence over them was rooted in reality; I had never softened nor palliated their faults; I had the loftiest motives, and had made every other end subordinate to that of spiritual growth. With a heartfelt blessing, I dismissed them; but none stirred and we all sat for some moments weeping. Then I went round the circle and bade each, separately, farewell (Fuller, 1852, pp. 179–180).

It should be noted that Fuller saw "spiritual growth" as the main aim of her teaching and her conception of this aim was rooted in the Transcendental view of soul. Capper concludes that her experience in Providence proved "her talents as a teacher" and "confirmed her commitment to female culture" (p. 251).

THE CONVERSATIONS

Fuller returned to Boston where she decided to hold "Conversations for a circle of women in Boston." Part of the motivation was financial, as she needed the income. The conversations were also her vehicle for developing "female culture.". Fuller found that there were many women in Boston who desired to read and discuss literature. Capper identifies three groups of women who came to Fuller's meetings. First, there were her close friends and former students such as Anna Barker and Caroline Sturgis. Then there was group of young women in their early twenties who were" "interested in new trends, socially active in Boston literary and reform circles, and, most important, although not intimate with her, ardently devoted to Margaret Fuller" (p. 291). In the third group were the wives of men involved in Transcendentalism or the abolitionist movement as well as writers and educators such as Elizabeth Peabody.

Capper notes that these women were highly educated for their times and were widely read in the classics. Most were multilingual. They were also religious liberals with the most leaning to some form of Transcendental-ism. Capper characterized the group as both a "feminine elite" and "avant-garde elite."

The meetings were held on the same day that Emerson lectured in the evening and were held in Elizabeth Peabody's home and what would later become her bookstore. Fuller charged 10 dollars for 13 two-hour meetings. Approximately, 30 women were usually in attendance. They were popular enough that Fuller ran them for almost 3 years.

The aim of these Conversations was to advance female culture by pro-viding a unique form of female education. She developed a prospectus that outlined her aims which was no less than changing the way women thought. This would be done by focusing on the "great questions—What were we born to do? How shall we do it?"

Capper concludes this was a highly original approach that combined both the Enlightenment focus on reason and inquiry combined with the Romantic focus on action.

She wrote that the most neglected aspect in educating women was that there was no opportunity for women to "reproduce" what they learned instead it was merely for "idle display." She opened the conversations with this statement:

> Women are now taught, at school, all that men are; they run over, superfi-cially, even more studies, without being really taught anything.... But, with this difference; men are called on from a very early period, to reproduce all that they learn. Their college exercises, their political duties, their profes-sional studies, and the first actions of life in any direction call on them to put to use what they have learned. But women learn without any attempt to reproduce. Their only reproduction is for the purposes of display. It is to sup-ply this defect ... that these conversations have been planned (cited in von Mehren, p. 115).

The model for the Conversations was based, in part, on Plato and Socratic dialogue. Fuller wrote Emerson before the Conversations that she was reading Plato "hoping to be tuned up thereby." The strongest influence though was the work of Alcott who had begun his conversations in eastern Massachusetts and had had some success. Alcott felt that lectures were too static while conversations were more fluid and spontaneous. Capper sug-gests that thus the Conversations "promoted originality and intellectual self-reliance" (p. 296).

Fuller felt that she was not "to *teach* any thing" but to "call ... out the thought of others" in the Conversations. She wrote in her journal: "The best that we receive from any thing can never be written. For it *is* not the positive amount of thought we have received, but the virtue that has flowed into us, and is now us, that is precious. If we can tell no one thought yet are higher, larger, wiser the work is done. The best part of life is too spiritual to bear recording." Ultimately, she felt that it is the "Spirit that must teach and help them to self impulse." Capper concludes that at its "deepest level" her approach was "mystical. It was in short, rather like Fuller herself" (p. 297).

Like the other Transcendentalists, Fuller (1992) believed that wisdom arises from the soul. She wrote, "You would not learn through facts of thought or action, but express through them the certainties of wisdom. In quietness yield thy soul to the casual soul" (p. 251). Her conversations could be seen as vehicles for activating the soul. "What woman needs is not to act or rule, but as nature to grow, as an intellect to discern, as a soul to live freely and unimpeded, to unfold such powers as were given her" (p. 261). Although written in the nineteenth century, the writing can still inspire. So maybe the motto for her conversations was what she wrote in *Woman for the Nineteenth Century*. "I believe that, at present, women are the best helpers of one another. *Let them think; let them act; let them know what they need* (Italics mine)" (pp. 344–345).

Unfortunately, there are no complete records of what transpired during the conversations. What we know most about them are from the records that Elizabeth Peabody kept along with recollections from participants. Capper notes three qualities regarding her speech. One was her command of the language and her ability to summarize the conversations. Another was the spontaneity of her speech, which helped create a sense of flow to the meetings. The third quality was her ability to listen and adjust her speech to the audience and the moment. In the second year, of the conversations, men were able to attend and Emerson notes that she was in "perfect tune with her company."

Although she would occasionally resort to lecture, most of the time was devoted to bringing the participants into the conversations. One participant commented that when someone spoke "Margaret knew how to seize the good meaning of it with hospitality and to make the speaker glad, and not sorry, that she had spoken" (cited in Capper, p. 299).

In the first meeting, Fuller found it difficult to get the women to speak but by the third meeting the women became more fully engaged. One woman who joined the conversations in the eighth meeting stated that the discussions had the quality of "a Platonic dialogue" but at the same time were not pedantic and had the tone "as simple as that of children in a school class" (p. 299). Fuller describes the conversations after the third meeting.

My class is singularly prosperous I think. I was so fortunate as to rouse at once the tone of simple earnestness which can scarcely, when once awakened, cease to vibrate. All seem in a glow and quite as receptive as I wish. They question and examine, yet follow leading; and thought (not opinions) have been trumps every time. There are about 25 members, and every one I believe took part with full interest. The first time, 10 members took part in the conversation; the last still more (Capper, pp. 299–300).

With regard to teaching strategies she would ask some of the participants to write short papers on next week's topic to help move the conversation forward. In the meetings, she sometimes would focus on definitions of terms such as "beauty" through Socratic questioning. By all accounts Fuller could be a very provocative questioner.

Her first series of meetings focused on Greek mythology which she saw as a vehicle for exploring some of the ideas of German idealism. In her view, these myths were examples of how material form reflected a deeper spirituality reality. Some of the women raised concerns about focusing on the paganism of the Greeks since many of the women were Christians. Fuller argued that history is more like a spiral than linear progression and that the Greeks reached full maturity while Western Christian civilization was still in its early stages.

In the remaining sessions, she focused on the Greek gods as symbols for different ideas: "Prometheus was made the type of Pure Reason; Jupiter, of Creative Energy or Will; Minerva, Intellectual Power or Practical Reason; and so on" (Capper, p. 302). This allowed her to play with ideas and explore such dualities as Apollo-Dionysius.

Fuller found that using the Greek myths in her first round of conversations allowed the participants to view their lives from a different lens. Once she said that "there is more Greek than Bostonian spoken at the meetings."

Capper believes that the second series of conversations that focused on the fine arts was more successful than the one on mythology. She used the term "poesy" which she took from Coleridge and Friedrich Schellling. She defined it in her journal "the expression of the sublime and beautiful, whether in measured words or in the fine arts. The human mind apprehending the harmony of the universe and making new combinations by its laws" (Capper, p. 304). This allowed Fuller to explore all the arts in the conversations.

The overall response to the conversations was positive although there were detractors who either reacted negatively to Fuller, or to the Transcendental ideas. One example of the positive reaction comes from one woman who wrote in her journal that

> I found myself in a new world of thought; a flood of light irradiated all that I had seen in nature, observed in life, or read in books. Whatever she spoke of revealed a hidden meaning, and everything seemed to be put in to true relation. Perhaps, I could best express it by saying that I was no longer the limitation of myself, but I felt the whole wealth of the universe open to me (Capper, p. 306).

The Conversations were Fuller's last experience as a teacher. However, she retained a strong interest in education the rest of her life. When she was working for the *New York Tribune* as a reporter and columnist, she saw the devastating effects of poverty. She advocated that all charitable institutions should have an educational component as she believed that education was central to social change. When she was in Paris, she visited the School for Idiots and was impressed by an innovative program where the children were taught carpentry as well as reading and math. She wrote a letter to the Tribune where she "recommended that Americans organize evening schools for working boys on the French model" (von Mehren, p. 244). In her role as a writer for the *Tribune,* she summarized her role as the promotion of "National Education by heightening and deepening the cultivation of individual minds, and the part which is assigned to Woman in the next stage of human progress in this country" (von Mehren, p. 229).

Fuller moved to Europe where she met her husband Giovanni Ossli with whom she had child. Tragically she, her husband and child drowned when their ship crashed during a storm off of Fire Island, New York. Fifty-one years later women, mostly in the women's suffrage movement, dedicated a plaque to her with the words "Author, Editor, Orator, Poet." Teacher could easily have been added to that plaque.

FULLER'S CONTRIBUTIONS TO EDUCATION

Educating Women

Margaret Fuller was a pioneer in women's education. Both in teaching children and adults her primary focus was raising the consciousness of women so that they would be more independent. It is clear that she affected the lives of the many women she taught in school and in her conversations. Her approach was within the Transcendentalist conception of self-culture. Emerson was a major influence as she once wrote that the "'mind is its own place,' was a dead phrase to me, till he cast light upon my mind" (Capper, p. 216). Murray (2008) notes that she also found appealing "Socrates admonition to each person to acquire self-understanding." She was drawn to Socrates idea that the person "live a virtuous life in accord with the form of the good that feels right" to the individual (p. 182).

Capper argues that her Conversations helped in the development of "organized American feminism" and directly influenced women such as Elizabeth Stanton in how they organized their meetings and activities. Many years after the conversations, Stanton believed that they were "the vindication of woman's right to think" (von Mehren, p. 119). It also contributed to a female counter-culture that was "self-critical" and "tough minded." Fuller was attempting to develop the self-culture of women that did not accept the norms that women were expected to adopt. Capper claims that through the conversations Fuller was "becoming antebellum America's foremost female activist of the mind" (p. 306).

Soul

Central to her vision of education was the soul. Again, this was important within the context of Transcendentalism, but she articulated her vision of soul in relation to women and their self-culture. For the Transcendentalists the soul was paramount. Fuller (1992) also saw it was the key to growth and self-culture.

> Religion was early awakened in my soul, a sense that what the soul is capable to ask it must attain, and that, though I might be aided and instructed by others, I must depend on myself as the only constant friend. This self dependence, which was honored in me, is deprecated as fault in most women. They are taught to learn their rule from without, not to unfold it from within. (p. 262)

In *Woman in the Nineteenth Century*, she writes passionately about the importance of soul.

Fuller's philosophy in a few words is "Being more a soul, she will not be less woman, for nature is perfected through spirit."(p. 347) Throughout this book she encourages women to listen and follow the wisdom of their own souls.

> Give the soul free course, let the organization of body and mind be freely developed, and the being will be fit for any and every relation to which it may be called. The intellect, no more than the sense of hearing, is to be cultivated merely that she may be a more valuable companion to man, but because the Power who gave a power, by its mere existence, signifies that it must be brought out toward perfection…. Let us be wise and not impede the soul. Let her work as she will. Let us have one creative energy, one incessant revelation. Let it take what form it will, and let us not bind it by the past to man or woman, black or white…. Let it be. (p. 298, p. 311)

So education was a way of nourishing and awakening the soul; without this any form of teaching and learning is inadequate. Today there is a growing movement in the area of spirituality in education (Palmer, 1998; Kessler, 2000; Miller, 2000) and Fuller's ideas resonates with this work. Fuller along with the other Transcendentalists developed a non-sectarian language about the soul that is helpful today. Soul is often connected to religion but Fuller and Emerson used the term in a manner that allows for an inclusive approach to spiritual education.

Holistic Perspective

For Fuller, human beings need to link the head and the heart. Her reference to the Muse and Minerva in *Woman in the Nineteenth Century* was her way of exploring her idea of the integrated individual. "What I mean by the Muse is the unimpeded clearness of the intuitive powers which a perfectly truthful adherence to every admonition of the higher instincts would bring to a finely organized human being" (p. 310).

Her call for women to more independent and to follow their own direction in life was the Minerva quality that she encouraged in women.

> It is therefore only in the present crisis that preference is given to Minerva. The power of continence must establish the legitimacy of freedom, the power of self-poise the perfection of motion…
>
> It is therefore that I would have woman lay aside all thought, such as she habitually cherishes of being taught and led by men. I would have her like the Indian girl, dedicate herself to the Sun, the Sun of Truth, and go no where if his beams did not make clear the path. I would have her free from compromise, from complaisance, from helplessness, because I would have her good enough and strong enough to love one and all beings, from the fullness, not the poverty of being. (pp. 311–312)

So again, Fuller frames her view of the integrated person in relation to women. To achieve the integration women needed to develop the Minerva side of themselves. This was what she emphasized as a teacher at all levels.

Fuller has given us a powerful vision of women that resonates today with educators who call for wholeness as a chief aim of education. Fuller developed complete vision of the person that includes the spiritual dimension as well as the intellectual and emotional aspects. Today when departments of education focus almost solely on a narrow economic perspective (e.g., competing in the global economy), Fuller's holistic vision deserves exploration and discussion.

Socratic Questioning

Fuller used Socratic questioning in teaching children and adults. The purpose was not to interrogate students but to draw out their inner wisdom. Unlike Bronson Alcott's conversations, which were recorded by Elizabeth Peabody, we do not have complete records of her interactions with her students. Yet, it is clear she was able to engage her students and the women in the conversations so that they became active participants in learning.

Journals

Fuller asked her students to keep journals. Journaling was seen as a key to the development of self-knowledge for the Transcendentalists and Fuller was no exception. Journals were a source of self-expression and occasionally students were asked to read from the journals to the whole class. Fuller once wrote her brother that she was pleased with how the journals were nurturing their "power of expression." It was through the journals of the students that we know something of the impact of her teaching. One student wrote, "She spoke upon what woman could do—said she should like to see a woman everything she might be, in intellect and character." (von Mehren, p. 102)

CONCLUSION

In her biography of Fuller, von Mehren concludes that "Teaching was natural to her, and she would, in fact never cease being a teacher in one guise or another.... As a teacher, tutor and translator, she played an important role ... in the development of a unique American culture—"an American mind"—a process that she prophesied would develop gradually out of the diversity of the American people" (p. 103, p. 351). Margaret Fuller left an important legacy as voice for and educator of women that continues to inspire. Jeffrey Steele writes: "After her death, however, left behind a legacy that led Elizabeth Cady Stanton and Susan B. Anthony to declare in their monumental *History of Woman Suffrage*, that she 'possessed more influence upon the thought of American women than any woman previous to her time'" (p. xlvi).

REFERENCES

Capper, C. (2002). *Margaret Fuller: An American Romantic Life. The private years*. New York: Oxford University Press.

Fuller, M. (1992). *The essential Margaret Fuller*. Jeffrey Steele (Ed.). New Brunswick, NJ: Rutgers University Press.

Fuller, M. (1852). *Memoirs of Margaret Fuller Ossili*. R. W. Emerson, W. H. Channing, & J. F. Clarke (Eds.). Boston: Phillips, Sampson.

Fuller, M. (1860). *Memoirs of Margaret Fuller Ossili*. R. W. Emerson, W. H. Channing, & J. F. Clarke (Eds.). Boston: Brown, Taggard and Chase.

Howe, D. W. (2007). *What hath God wrought: The transformation of America, 1815–1848*. Oxford: Oxford University Press.

Kessler, R. (2000). *The soul of education: Helping students find connection, compassion, and character at school*. Alexandria, VA: Association for Supervision and Curriculum Development.

Miller, J. (2000). *Education and the soul: Toward a spiritual curriculum*. Albany, NY: SUNY Press.

Murray, M. M. (2008). *Margaret Fuller: Wandering pilgrim*. Athens, GA: University of Georgia Press.

Myerson, J. (Ed.). (2008). *Fuller in her own time: A biographical chronicle of her life, drawn from recollections, Interviews, and Memoirs by Family, Friends, and Associates*. Iowa City: University of Iowa Press.

Palmer, P. (1998). *The courage to teach: Exploring the inner landscape of a teacher's life*. San Francisco, CA: Jossey-Bass.

von Mehren, J. (1994) *Minerva and the Muse: The life of Margaret Fuller*. Amherst, MA: University of Massachusetts Press.

CHAPTER 5

HENRY THOREAU: ENVIRONMENTAL EDUCATOR

"I believe in the forest, and in the meadow, and in the night in which the corn grows."

Henry David Thoreau is the most well known of the five individuals discussed in this book. Lewis Hyde in his introduction to a collection of Thoreau's essays writes that "Thoreau is arguably the original American ecologist" (p. xxvii). His book *Walden* has sold millions of copies around the world and his essay on civil disobedience has inspired several generations to nonviolent change. During his life he was engaged in many activities including surveying, pencil making, teaching and writing. He saw himself mostly as a writer; when he was 32, he wrote, "I have chosen letters as my profession" (Thoreau, 1958, p. 249). However, in his 20s he actively sought a career as a teacher and throughout his life he commented on education and learning. Thoreau was a learner throughout his life. Richardson (1986) in his book on Thoreau writes about this quality near the end of his life:

> Thoreau's nearly limitless capacity for being interested is one of the most unusual and attractive things about him. That his interests were still expanding, his wonders still green, his capacity for observation, expression and connection still growing is the most impressive evidence possible that his spirits this January were still on the wing (p. 376).

Trancendental Learning: The Educational Legacy of Alcott, Emerson, Fuller, Peabody and Thoreau, pp. 59–73

His continued interest in observation, knowing and learning can contribute enormously to our understanding of holistic education and particularly environmental education.

YOUTH AND TEACHING CAREER

Thoreau was born and died in Concord. Although he did travel to places such as Maine and Minnesota, Concord was the center of his life. He never tired of walking in the woods and fields surrounding the town and observing nature. His family included his father, who was a pencil maker, and Henry occasionally helped in his father's factory. His mother bore three other children besides Henry and he was close to his brother John. As a child he slept in a trundle bed with John. In Harding's biography of Thoreau he writes of Henry's early fascination with the universe.

> John would go to sleep at once, but Henry often lay awake. When his mother once found him so, she asked, "Why Henry dear, don't you go to sleep?" "Mother," he replied, "I have been looking through the stars to see if I could see God behind them" (cited in Harding, p. 12).

The family was close and Thoreau spent much of his life in the family home. He and John attended school at the Concord Academy. One of the few surviving papers from the school is one by Henry written when he was about 11 or 12. The paper is entitled "The Seasons" and in it Thoreau describes each of the four seasons. Here is his description of summer. "Next comes Summer. Now we see a beautiful sight. The trees and flowers are in bloom. Now is the pleasantest part of the year. Now the fruit begins to form on the trees and all things look beautiful" (Harding, p. 27).

After graduating from the Academy, Henry attended Harvard College, which at that time had only 250 students. At the Academy and Harvard Henry studied Greek and Latin and the classics. Although he was critical of his education at Harvard where there were "all the branches of learning there but not the roots" (Harding, p. 51), his education can be seen in much of his writing. In *Walden* and other works he continually makes references to the ancients, and he read many of their works in the original Greek and Latin. The library at Harvard was also a boon. Throughout his life Thoreau was a voracious reader and he benefited greatly from access to all the books there. Another important influence at Harvard was Edward Tyrrell Channing, who taught English composition, and Thoreau admitted that through his instruction he first learned to express himself in writing.

At that time, Thoreau graduated from Harvard there were four professions open to college graduates—the ministry, law, medicine or teaching. Harding states that Thoreau did not hesitate in choosing teaching as many

individuals in his family had been teachers. He was offered a job immediately at the Center School in Concord. However, his stay there was short.
After 2 weeks one of the members of the school committee came by and
said to Thoreau that he should use corporal punishment to discipline the
students. Thoreau immediately walked back into the school and hit several
students. The same evening he resigned his teaching position since he
could not abide this approach to disciplining children.

Thoreau continued to seek teaching positions in New England, but because
of his lack of experience he was not successful. During the fall of 1837, his
friendship with Emerson developed. Emerson opened his library to
Thoreau and they spent time walking together. Emerson's thought and
particularly his book *Nature* had a strong impact on Thoreau. It was also
Emerson who encouraged Thoreau to start a journal. Thoreau kept a journal throughout his life; in his later years it includes his major insights since
he did not publish any books after *Walden*.

Thoreau was invited to a group called the "Hedge Club" (Chapter 1,
"Intellectual Roots"). Named after Henry Hedge, this group included
George Ripley, Margaret Fuller, Orestes Brownson, Bronson Alcott, Theodore Parker, Elizabeth Peabody, Christopher Cranch, John Sullivan Dwight
and Emerson. This club attracted the attention of others including the
newspapers and the members of the club were referred to as "Transcendentalists." As its youngest member, Thoreau was exposed to the ideas of Transcendentalism and he engaged these ideas such as the importance of the
individual conscience the rest of his life.

The Concord Academy

In June 1838, Thoreau opened his own school. In February, he was able
to enlist his brother to teach as well in the new school called The Concord
Academy. This school was a success as enrollment reached 25 and eventually included Louisa May Alcott as one of its students.

The school day began with prayers and then a short talk by one of the
brothers. One talk was on the change of the seasons and it was reported
that the students were transported by Henry's story telling. There were two
rooms with John teaching downstairs where he instructed the students in
English and math. Upstairs Henry taught Latin, Greek, French, physics,
natural philosophy, and natural history.

Harding states that the school was "noted for its innovations" (p. 82). It
employed the principle of learning by doing as the students went on field
trips around Concord and Henry was able to demonstrate his knowledge of
the flowers and animals. Once he picked up a plant that was miniscule, and
with a magnifying glass, showed the students a tiny blossom. Through these
trips he was able to show his delight in nature thus hopes to inspire in his

students a similar joy. One of his entries in his journal (1961) at this time conveys this joy he felt.

> It is a luxury to muse by a wall-side in the sunshine of September afternoon-to cuddle down under a gray stone, and hearken to the siren song of the cricket. Day and night seem henceforth but accidents and the time is always a still eventide, and as the close of a happy day. Parched fields and mulleins gilded with the slanting rays are my diet. I know of no word so fit to express this disposition of Nature as *Alma Natura*. (p. 7).

The field trips were also opportunities to discover the natural history of the area. Sanborn (1917) describes one of these activities in his early biography of Thoreau.

> Henry Thoreau called attention to a spot on the rivershore, where he fancied the Indians had made their fires, and perhaps had a fishing village.... "Do you see," said Henry, "anything here that would be likely to attract Indians to this spot?" One boy said, "Why, here is the river for their fishing"; another pointed to the woodland near by, which could give them game. "Well, is there anything else?" pointing out a small rivulet that must come, he said, from a spring not far off, which could furnish water cooler than the river in the summer; and a hillside above it that would keep off the north and northwest wind in winter. Then, moving inland a little farther, and looking carefully about, he struck his spade several times, without result. Presently, when the boys began to think their young teacher and guide was mistaken, his spade struck a stone. Moving forward a foot or two, he set his space in again, stuck another stone, and began to dig in a circle. He soon uncovered the red, fire-marked stones of the long-disused Indian fireplace; thus proving that he had been right in his conjecture. Having settled the point, he carefully covered up his find and replaced the turf—not wishing to have the domestic altar of the aborigines profaned by mere curiosity (pp. 205–206).

Other activities included going to the local newspaper and watching the setting of the type. The brothers also had the land plowed so that the students could plant crops in their own individual plots. He also had the students do some surveying as way to see the practical application of mathematics. The brothers extended the recess from the usual 10 min to 30 min to allow the students more freedom. Another example of how relaxed the brothers were with the students is when Henry and John put tar on their boat, the students watched them and played in the shallow water (Harding, p. 83).

The school ran for 3 years and was closed on April 1, 1841, when John's health started to fail. Harding writes that "The pupils remembered the schools and its teachers with "affection," "gratitude," and "enthusiasm." One of the students, Benjamin Lee, thought he would never forget the kindness and goodwill of the Thoreau brothers "in their great desire to impress upon the minds of their scholars to do right always" (p. 86) Harding goes on to assert that:

> The Thoreau school was a century ahead of its time. Granted Bronson Alcott's famous Temple School had anticipated some of its innovations by a few years, but Alcott with his experimentation had brought the wrath of the community down on his head. The Thoreau's, on the other hand, although many of their innovations were more radical than those of Alcott, won acceptance and made of their school a considerable and memorable success (p. 86).

John died in early 1842. The death of his brother and closest friend was devastating for Thoreau. Yet, Richardson argues that after a period of illness and mourning, Thoreau gained a sense of freedom that led to creative output in his writing. The death of Emerson's young son, Waldo, who was close to Thoreau also seemed to spark a sense of urgency and self-discovery.

WALDEN

Thoreau's 2-year stay at Walden pond and the book that resulted from that period were defining marks in Thoreau's life. Richardson writes that Thoreau produced the greatest amount of quality writing during his stay there.

Emerson owned the land on which Thoreau built his small cabin. Thoreau went to Walden for several reasons (Richardson, 1986). First, he wanted independence, as outside of his years at Harvard, he had always lived with either his family or at Emerson's. Second it was a statement of social reform. This was a time when communal living was popular with projects such as Brook Farm and Fruitlands; in contrast, Thoreau wanted to explore a smaller, simpler form of living. Finally, Walden was an effort to meet life on its most basic terms and through this process awaken. Thoreau (1961) liked to use the image of morning as a metaphor for this awakening.

> The morning, which is the most memorable season of the day is the awakening hour.... All memorable events, I should say, transpire in morning time and in a morning atmosphere. The Vedas say, "All intelligences awake with the morning." Poetry and art, and the fairest and most memorable of the actions of men, date from such an hour. (p. 134)

It is significant that Thoreau quotes from the Vedas to make his point, as the connection is made to the Eastern concept of liberation. When the Buddha was asked who he was, he said "I am awake." Thoreau also saw awakening as a central aim of life and of education.

Thoreau had been introduced to Eastern thought through Emerson and his library, which contained several works such as the *Bhagavad Gita*. Harding and others have noted that he connected more with these writings than those from the Judeo-Christian tradition. Thoreau (1961) wrote in his journal that he liked "Brahma, Hari, Buddha, the Great Spirit, as well as God" (p. 35). One aspect of Eastern thought that he was drawn to was contemplation and solitude. At Walden, he (1986) was able to practice his own form of contemplation as he sat in front of his cottage.

> I sat in my sunny doorway from sunrise till noon, rapt in a revery, amidst the pines and hickories and sumachs, in undisturbed solitude and stillness, while the birds sang around or flitted noiseless through the house, until by the sun falling in at my west window, or the noise of some traveller's wagon on the highway, I was reminded of the lapse of time. I grew in those seasons like corn in the night, and they were far better than any work of the hands would have been. They were not time subtracted from my life, but so much over and above my usual allowance. I realized what the Orientals mean by contemplation and the forsaking of works. For the most part, I minded not how the hours went. (p. 157)

Thoreau kept in touch with his former students and they came to visit him at Walden. One student wrote:

> We boys used to visit him on Saturday afternoons at his house by Walden and he would show us interesting things in the woods nearby.... He was never stern or pedantic but natural and very agreeable and friendly, but a person you would never feel inclined to fool with. (Harding, 1982, p. 194)

Walden is meant to inspire the individual to awaken and to live the life they can imagine. Thoreau encourages us to "hear a different drummer." Walden is read in many high school classrooms but one wonders whether the educational system with its emphasis on standardization actually undermines this inspiring vision.

CIVIL DISOBEDIENCE

This paper was first published under the title "Resistance to Civil Government" in 1849 in Elizabeth Peabody's *Aesthetic Papers*. It was reprinted in 1866 after his death with the title "Civil Disobedience." The context for this essay was the Mexican war and the institution of slavery; Thoreau strongly opposed both. In 1846, Thoreau spent one night in the Concord jail because he refused to pay the poll tax. He was released the next morning when an anonymous person paid the tax; Harding speculates that it was his Aunt Maria who came forward. People were interested in why Thoreau took this action so he first delivered a lecture on the theme of resistance in 1848, which eventually was published as the essay in Peabody's book.

Thoreau (1986) was not an anarchist and argued for better government rather than no government (p. 386). The main argument of the essay is for the supremacy of the individual conscience. He writes, "Must the citizen ever for a moment, or in the least degree, resign his conscience to the legislator? Why has every man a conscience, then? I think that we should be men first, and subjects afterward" (p. 387). In referring to the soldier, Thoreau argues that "The mass of men serve the state thus, not as men mainly, but as machines, with their bodies" (p. 388).

To counter the machinery of the state people may have to break the law. Thoreau writes that if the state makes you "an agent of injustice" then "break the law." He adds, "Under a government which imprisons any unjustly, the true place for a just man is also a prison" (p. 398). These phrases have inspired the followers of Gandhi and King to break unjust laws and become imprisoned. To the many others who have read this essay it asks them to search their own conscience and view their decisions within a powerful ethical framework. This is an essay which should be required reading in a democratic society.

TRANSCENDENTAL NATURALIST

As Thoreau matured into his mid to later 30s, he took more and more interest in science and the observation of nature. His later journals are filled with his observation of nature that he gathered on his walks around Concord. He wrote in his journal that he found himself "inspecting little granules, as it were, on the bark of trees and I call it studying lichens"(p. 81). These walks were precious to him and he wrote in his journal that much preferred to walk alone. He wrote, "They do not consider that the wood-path and the boat are my studio, where I maintain a sacred solitude and cannot admit promiscuous company.... Ask me for a certain number of dollars if you will, but do not ask be for my afternoons" (cited in Harding, 1982, p. 292).

As mentioned earlier, Thoreau read widely throughout his life and was influenced by many naturalists and scientists including Goethe, Darwin, Agassiz, and Linnaeus. Richardson (1986) notes that Linneaus wrote about the creative forces of nature and that the "whole earth is alive, not inert" (p. 255). Echoing this idea, Thoreau (1986) wrote in *Walden*:

> The earth is not a mere fragment of dead history, stratum upon stratum like the leaves of a book, to be studied by geologists and antiquaries chiefly, but living poetry like the leaves of a tree, which precede flowers and fruit—not a fossil earth, but a living earth; compared with whose central life all animal and vegetable life is merely parasitic. (p. 357)

There are hints here of the Gaia hypothesis that suggests that entire earth is a living organism with its own intelligence. In his journal, Thoreau (1961) wrote that science "sees everywhere the traces, and it is itself the agent, of a Universal Intelligence" (p. 125). Although in his later years Thoreau focused on detail, it was always against the background that nature operated according to universal principles. The human mind also reflects these universal principles. In writing about husbandry from the ancients to his time, he writes about the "perennial mind" which does not change from one year to another. The "perennial mind" is that deep wisdom within the individual that is in harmony with nature.

He was a pantheist and saw the divine in nature. He wrote in one paper that "It [a pine tree] is as immortal as I am and perchance will go to as high a heaven, there to tower above me still ... " (cited in Harding, 1982, p. 393). This phrase was struck from the essay by the editor, James Russell Lowell, apparently because of it pantheistic overtones. Thoreau was enraged by this editing and wrote a strong letter to Lowell protesting. Lowell never responded to Thoreau's letter and went ahead publishing it without the sentence in the *Atlantic Monthly*. Thoreau was never afraid to share his beliefs about nature and was rightly angered when someone deleted a statement of his vision.

Bronson Alcott (1872) was a good friend of Thoreau and in his book *Concord Days* he quotes Thoreau's statement about going out on a spring day. It is a beautiful description of Thoreau's reverence for nature:

> This afternoon I throw off my outside coat, a mild spring day. I must hie me to the meadows. The air is full of bluebirds. The ground is almost entirely bare. The villagers are in the sun and every man is happy whose work takes him out-of-doors. I go by Sleepy Hollow towards the great fields. I lean over a rail to hear what is in the air, liquid with the bluebird's warble. My life partakes of infinity. The air is deep as our natures. Is the drawing in of this vital air attended with no more glorious results than I witness? The air is a velvet cushion against which I press my ear. I go forth to make new demands on life. I wish to begin this summer well. To do something in it worthy and wise. To transcend my daily routine and that of my townsmen, to have my immortality now, that it be in the quality of my daily life.... May I dare as I have never done. May I purify myself anew as with fire and water, soul and body. May my melody not be wanting to the season. May I gird myself to a hunter of the beautiful, that nought escape me. May I attain to a youth never attained. I am eager to report the glory of the universe: may I be worthy to do it; to have got through regarding human values, so as not to be distracted from regarding divine values. (pp. 263–264)

This is one of my favorite passages in all of Thoreau's writing. If there was anyone who was worthy of reporting "the glory of the universe" it was Thoreau. His walks in nature were a "partaking of infinity." Through this partaking he would encounter "divine values" to inspire his spiritual growth.

In 1855, Frank Sanborn opened a new school in Concord. He asked Thoreau to lecture at his school once a week and but Thoreau was concerned that it would take away from his other tasks. Sanborn took the students on weekly excursions around Concord and occasionally Thoreau would join them. One student, Samuel Higginson (1862) recalled Thoreau.

> He was ... to us more than a charming companion; he became our instructor, full of wisdom and consideration, patiently listening to our crude ideas of Nature's laws and to our juvenile philosophy, not without a smile, yet in a moment ready to correct and set us right again. And so in the afternoon walk, or the long holiday jaunt, he opened to our unconscious eyes a thousand beauties of the earth and air, and taught us to admire and appreciate all that was impressive and beautiful in the natural world around us. When with him, objects before so tame acquired new life and interest. We saw no beauty in the note of veery or wood—thrush until he pointed out to us their sad yet fascinating melancholy. He turned our hearts toward every flower, revealing to us the haunts of rhodora and arethusa ...
>
> His ear was keenly alive to musical sounds, discriminating with astonishing accuracy between the notes of various songsters. This discernment enabled him to distinguish at once the songs of many birds singing together, selecting each one with great nicety of perception. A single strain was enough for him to recall the note at once, and he always had some English translation, or carefully marked paraphrase of it, singularly expressive and unique. (pp. 11–12)

In reading Thoreau's journals one cannot help be struck by his sensitivity to sound and love of music. He refers to ethereal music or what he calls "fine Aeolian harp music" that permeates the air. But he also found music in the birds and crickets and even in the hoe striking the stone. All of the sounds transported Thoreau. He wrote, "When I hear music I fear no danger, I am invulnerable, I see no foe. I am related to the earliest times and to the latest.... It releases me; it bursts my bonds" (p. 171).

Synthesis

Recent research on Thoreau has found that in his last years that he was integrating his inquiries in nature with science, literature and philosophy to form a "comprehensive theory of the process of nature's variation and development ... the pursuit of the knowledge of a single thing became the unceasing quest to comprehend the encompassing unity of all things" (Robinson, pp. 177–178). Robinson argues that Thoreau's work focused on an ever-enlarging network of relations, which natural objects were defined through their part in a larger system, and thus through the process of their interactions. In accord with his long-held faith that the study of nature was intimately connected with the culture of the self, Thoreau believed that this ever-enlarging system of relations also included human consciousness and human agency. (p. 184)

Thoreau was seeking what he called "Beautiful Knowledge." Thoreau (2002) wrote: "The highest that we can attain to is not Knowledge, but Sympathy with Intelligence" (p. 172). His metaphor is the "lighting up of the mist by the sun." Thoreau used the sun as an image of that Intelligence which is the source of "Beautiful Knowledge." At the end of the essay "Walking" he writes:

> So we saunter toward the Holy Land, till one day the sun shall shine more brightly than ever he has done, shall perchance shine into our minds and ears, and light up our whole lives with a great awakening light, as warm and serene and golden as on a bankside in autumn. (p. 177)

Although the closure of the Concord Academy was the end of Thoreau's teaching career, he wrote about education and learning throughout his life. Some of the entries in his journal toward the end of his life are about education. For example, he wrote this in 1859 about two and a half years before he died. "How vain to try to teach youth, or anybody truths! They can only learn them after their own fashion, and when they get ready" (p. 212). Thoreau was anticipating educators like A S Neill and Carl Rogers with such thoughts.

THOREAU'S CONTRIBUTION TO EDUCATION

Environmental Education

Thoreau can be seen as the first environmental educator. First, there was the work he did in Concord Academy with the field trips into nature. He continued this work in Sanborn's school as well.

Walden and his other writings have inspired environmentalists and conservationists for over 150 years. One of today's leading environmental educators, David Orr (1992), writes this about Thoreau.

> *Walden* is a model of the possible unity between personhood, pedagogy and place. For Thoreau, Walden was more than his location. It was a laboratory for observation and experimentation; a library of data about geology, history,

flora and fauna; a source of inspiration and renewal; and a testing ground for the man. *Walden* is no monologue; it is a dialogue between a man and place. In sense, *Walden* wrote Thoreau. His genius, I think was to allow himself to be shaped by his place to allow it to speak with his voice. (p. 126)

Unlearning

Thoreau was an advocate of letting go of our previous learning so that we can see clearly. One of the early entries in his journal describes this process:

As the least drop of wine tinges the whole goblet, so the least particle of truth colors our whole life. It is never isolated, or simply added as treasure to our stock. When any real progress is made, we unlearn and learn anew what we thought we knew before. (p. 3)

He (1961) continued this theme throughout his life and towards the end of life he wrote this in his journal:

It is only when we forget all our learning that we begin to know. I do not get nearer by a hair's breadth to any natural object so long as I presume that I have an introduction to it from some learned man. To conceive of it with a total apprehension I must for the thousandth time approach it as something totally strange. If you would make acquaintance with the ferns you must forget your botany. (p. 210)

One is reminded of Eastern approaches to learning; for example, Suzuki (1970) said that we need a *beginner's mind* to see things as they really are.

Learning by Doing

I have already cited Harding's comment on Thoreau's pedagogy which focused on learning by doing rather than listening to lectures. In *A Week on the Concord and Merrimack Rivers* (1980) he wrote "Knowledge is to acquire only by a corresponding experience. How can we *know* what we are *told* merely?" (p. 365).

Thoreau gives an example of learning by doing in *Walden*. He asserts students should not just study life but *live* it from beginning to end. "Which would have advanced the most at the end of a month—the boy who had made his own jackknife from the ore which had dug and smelted, reading as much as would be necessary for this—or the boy who attended the lectures on metallurgy" (pp. 94–95).

Embodied Knowing

In his eulogy on Thoreau, Emerson (2003) commented on how important physical activity was in his life, "there was a wonderful fitness of body and mind.... The length of his walk uniformly made the length of his writing. If shut up in the house, he did not write at all" (p. 460). Thoreau himself wrote "A man thinks as well though his legs and arms as his brain. We exaggerate the importance and exclusiveness of the headquarters" (p. 212). Transcendental learning cannot be just a head trip, it must be rooted in our bodies as well.

The senses are the way into what Thoreau called the natural life. He (1980) wrote, "We pray for no higher heaven than the pure senses can furnish, purely sensuous life" (p. 379). For Thoreau, the senses were ways to connect to the divine. "The ears are made, not for such trivial uses as men are wont to suppose, but to hear celestial sounds. The eyes were not made for such groveling put to and worn out by, but to behold beauty now invisible. May we not see God" (p. 382). Thoreau then called for an education of the senses. "What is it, then to educate but develop these divine germs called the senses?" (p. 382).

However, Thoreau was not a materialist. He encouraged inquiry into what he called the "OTHER WORLD which the instinct of mankind has so long predicted".... He felt that "Menu, Zoroaster, Socrates, Christ, Shakespeare, Swedenborg" were the "astronomers" of that world that could guide in that inquiry (p. 386).

Holistic Learning

Thoreau believed that writing and learning should involve the whole person. In his journal (1861) he wrote.

> We cannot write well or truly but what we write with gusto. The body, the senses, must conspire with the mind. Expression is the act of the whole man, that our speech may be vascular. The intellect is powerless to express thought without the aid of the heart and liver and every member. Often I feel that my head stands out too dry, when it should be immersed. A writer, a man writing, is the scribe of all nature; he is the corn and the grass and the atmosphere writing. It is always essential that we love to do what we are doing, do it with a heart. (p. 57)

Thoreau (2002) once wrote, "Surely joy is the condition of life" (p. 5). We can assume that he saw learning also as essentially a joyful act and happiness as goal of education.

Community as the School

Thoreau believed that learning should not be limited to the school building but that the entire community should participate in the children's education. In *Walden* he makes the call for "uncommon schools" so that "villages were universities" (p. 154). Like Alcott and Fuller, he also believed that learning should continue throughout our adult lives.

Contemplation

Just as community was important in learning, solitude and silence were also fundamental to Thoreau. He (1980) wrote, "As the truest society approaches always nearer to solitude, so the most excellent speech finally falls into Silence. Silence is audible to all men, at all times, and in all places. She is when we hear inwardly, sound when we hear outwardly" (p. 391). Silence and solitude are conducive to contemplation. In his journal (1961), Thoreau described contemplation in more detail:

> I must walk more with free senses. It is as bad to *study* stars and clouds as flowers and stones. I must let my senses wander as my thoughts, my eyes see without looking.... Be not preoccupied with looking. Go not to the object; let it come to you. When I have found myself ever looking down and confining my gaze to the flowers, I have thought it might be well to get into the habit of observing the clouds as a corrective; but no! that study would be just as bad. What I need is not to look at all, but a true sauntering of the eye. (p. 99)

Contemplation, in Thoreau's view, allows the person to *be* with an object rather than become a subject observing an object. This way of knowing is generally ignored in education but needs to be included if we are truly to have a more holistic approach to learning.

Relationship with Students

When Thoreau was searching for a teaching position, he wrote Orestes Brownson about his vision of teaching.

> I would make education a pleasant thing both to the teacher and scholar. This discipline, which we allow to be the end of life, should not be one thing in the schoolroom and another in the street. We should seek to be fellow students with the pupil, and we should learn of as well as with him, if we would be most helpful to him. (Harding, 1982, p. 55)

The comments from former pupils cited earlier would indicate that Thoreau treated his students with respect and care. Although he could be difficult in his relationships with adults, he enjoyed being with children. Throughout his life Thoreau loved demonstrating nature's beauty and wonder to children. When Thoreau died, school was dismissed and many children in Concord attended the funeral.

Love

Like Gandhi and King, Thoreau saw love as the fundamental force in the cosmos. He (2002) wrote: "Love is the wind, the tide, the waves, the sunshine. It never ceases, it never slacks; it can move the globe without a resting-place; it can warm without fire; it can feed without meat; it can clothe without garments; it can shelter without roof" (p. 60). Thoreau would agree with King when he wrote that love "is at the center of the cosmos. It is the great unifying force of life." Yet, Thoreau despairs that love has been "but meanly and sparingly applied" to social ends. Thus, he encourages us to "get your living by loving" (p. 201).

I have written about how the kind of love that Thoreau and King speak can be integrated into schools and educational settings. The aim is eventually to build what Kind called the "Beloved Community" which focuses both love and justice (Miller, 2009).

I close this chapter with a quotation from a letter to Harrison Blake with whom Thoreau carried on a life-long correspondence:

> Do what you love. Know your own bone; gnaw at it bury it, unearth it, and gnaw it still. Do not be too moral. You may cheat yourself out of much life so. Aim above morality. Be not *simply* good—be good for something. All fables indeed have their morals, but the innocent enjoy the story.
>
> Let nothing come between you and the light. (Thoreau, Letters p. 38)

We can be thankful that Thoreau let himself stand in the light.

REFERENCES

Alcott, A. B. (1872). *Concord days*. Boston: Roberts Brothers.

Emerson, R. W. (2003). *Selected writings of Ralph Waldo Emerson*. New York, NY: Signet.

Harding, W. (1982). *The days of Henry Thoreau: A biography*. New York, NY: Dover.

Higginson, S. S. (1862). Henry D. Thoreau in *Harvard Magazine*. VIII: 313–318.

Miller, J. P. (2009). Eros and education. In M. Sousza, et al. (Eds.), *International handbook of education for spirituality, care, and wellbeing*. New York, NY: Springer.

Orr, D. (1992). *Ecological literacy: Education and the transition to a postmodern world*. Albany, NY: SUNY Press.

Richardson, R. D. (1986). *Henry David Thoreau: A life of the mind*. Berkeley, CA: University of California Press.

Robinson, D. M. (2004). *Natural life: Thoreau's worldly transcendentalism*. Ithaca, NY: Cornell University Press.

Sanborn, F. B. (1917). *The Life of Henry David Thoreau*. Boston: Houghton Mifflin.

Suzuki, S. (1970). *Zen mind, beginner's mind*. New York, NY: Weatherhill.

Thoreau, H. D. (1958). *Correspondence*. W. Harding & Carl Bode (Eds.). New York, NY: New York University Press.

Thoreau, H. D. (1961). Shepard, O. (Ed.). *The heart of Thoreau's journals*. New York, NY: Dover.

Thoreau, H. D. (1980). *A Week on the Concord and Merrimack rivers*. Princeton, NJ: Princeton University Press.

Thoreau, H. D. (1986). *Walden and civil disobedience*. New York, NY: Penguin.

Thoreau, H. D. (2002). "Walking" *The essay of Henry Thoreau*. New York, NY: North Point Press.

Thoreau, H. D. (2004). *Letters to a spiritual seeker*. New York, NY: W.W. Norton.

Note: Much of this chapter entitled "Thoreau: Holistic Educator and Environmental Education" appeared in *Social Ecology: Applying ecological understanding to our lives and our planet* (2011) D. Wright, C. E. Camden-Pratt, & S. B. Hill, (Eds.). Stroud, UK: Hawthorn Press. www.hathornpress.com

CHAPTER 6

ELIZABETH PEABODY: EDUCATIONAL REFORMER

"Everything in education depends on the view taken of the soul."

Like Bronson Alcott, Elizabeth Peabody devoted her life to education. Bruce Ronda (1999) in his biography of Peabody states that "education was her great calling and her grand passion" (p. 7) Elizabeth (1841) wrote: "The education both of old and young has always been my hobby; indeed, life always appears to me as an education, and is more interesting in this view of it, than in any other" (p. 7). She taught in several schools and helped Alcott in the Temple School, which she wrote about in *Record of a School*. Her crowning achievement was being an advocate for kindergarten. Influenced by the work of Freidrich Froebel, Peabody argued that emphasis in kindergarten should be on play rather than academic work. Ronda (1999) writes:

> The kindergarten was her greatest work, her *Nature, Walden,* "Song of Myself," *Woman in the Nineteenth Century*. Like those works, Peabody's version of kindergarten was the self writ large, a summary and recapitulation of her life as she understood it. The movement reflected all the influences in her life and career: her mother's school and philosophy; the impact of Channing's affective Unitarianism: the Transcendentalist protest and the larger Romantic ideology; her devotion to history; and her emphasis on the self in the social order. (p. 307)

Trancendental Learning: The Educational Legacy of Alcott, Emerson,
Fuller, Peabody and Thoreau: pp. 75–87
Copyright © 2011 by Information Age Publishing
All rights of reproduction in any form reserved.

Ronda asserts that Peabody was a "practical intellectual," who needed to see ideas actualized; for her education allowed for this actualization through interaction between self and society. Ronda compares the work of Peabody to Paulo Freire since both saw education as "liberating praxis." Ronda suggests that Freire follows the precedent set by Peabody "for the act of teaching necessarily requires some reflection on the theory and implications, which in turn informs the daily classroom work" (p. 4).

EARLY INFLUENCES

Elizabeth grew up in a large family. Her younger sisters, Mary and Sophia, were well known through their marriages to Horace Mann and Nathaniel Hawthorne, respectively. She also had three brothers. Elizabeth was deeply influenced by her mother, who was a teacher and ran her own school. Mrs Peabody taught in several schools that were attached to her homes in Massachusetts. Elizabeth attended her mother's school in Salem where the curriculum was rigorous with a focus on history and literature. Students read the *Illiad* and the *Odyssey*, as well as material from Chaucer and Spenser. Ronda (1999) notes that Mrs Peabody did not modify the curriculum for the girls and offered the same curricula as "boys would receive at a college preparatory academy" (p. 41). Her mother also used innovative teaching methods; for example, she had the students write imaginary letters home from countries they had just studied. (Marhshall, p. 83). Her mother also gave her students the work of female authors since she believed that women were to be the guardians of culture. Clearly, she presented a strong model for Elizabeth as she pursued her career. Her father was physician and dentist, but was not much of a factor in Elizabeth's intellectual and emotional life, as he struggled financially throughout his life.

William Ellery Channing, a Unitarian Minister, was another important influence on Elizabeth. Elizabeth was only seven when her mother took her to hear Channing preach. At that young age Elizabeth was moved by Channing's presence and his message, which was counter to the Calvinist idea that human beings were depraved and sinful. (see Chapter 1). For Channing, perfection was possible through *knowledge, love* and *activity*. Marshall (2005) claims that "No one could have stated more concisely the aims that would propel Elizabeth to adulthood" (p. 72). When Elizabeth was 13, she had a chance to have a personal interview with Channing where she asked questions and fully engaged the minister in conversation. This meeting confirmed her admiration for Channing.

It was ten years later, when Elizabeth was 27, she become close to Channing. She found his presence empowering and she wrote that he seemed to connect with her soul like a "strain of soft but irresistably persuasive music which even before you are aware it affects you has carried captive all your feelings" (Peabody, 1984, p. 53). They met frequently to discuss ideas; Channing introduced Elizabeth to Wordsworth and Coleridge and they discussed that latter's use of the word *transcendental*. Channing (2006) believed that "the idea of God, sublime and awful as it is, is the idea of our own spiritual nature, purified and enlarged to infinity. In ourselves are the elements of Divinity" (p. 15). This idea, of course, was at the core of transcendentalism and inspired Elizabeth in her view of education. She was inspired to write Wordsworth and share some her ideas about education. She felt that presently "the whole theory of education was defective ... that the soul was neglected" (Marshall, p. 165). She also encouraged Wordsworth to write a book of poetry for children.

The work of Richard Lovell Edgeworth, and his daughter Maria Edgeworth, with their book *Essays on Practical Education* were another major influence on Elizabeth's approach to education. The Edgeworths' believed that young children's senses should be stimulated and that learning can be enhanced through working with simple toys and clay or wax for modeling (Ronda, p. 86). What was lacking in the Edgeworths' vision was the moral and spiritual. She wrote that children carry "Paradise" within their breasts and this needs to be honored and nurtured. Ronda (1999) writes: "The real issue, she was coming to see, was the training of the whole person, shaping not just the intellect but also the moral and spiritual sensibility, together with a sense of collective identity of belonging not simply to oneself or one's family but to the entire human race" (p. 87).

TEACHING

Elizabeth began teaching at the age of 17 when the family moved to Lancaster, Massachusetts. Her goal from the beginning was "educating children morally and spiritually as well as intellectually" (Peabody, 1841, p. 40). The classroom was attached to the Peabody home and included 11 students. Of 11, five were her siblings. The other students were daughters of farmers and traders.

One of Elizabeth's life-long passions was history so that her curriculum included studies of Greece and Rome, discovery of the New World and the history of New England. To stimulate reading, she asked the students to bring in books that they enjoyed and to read them aloud in class. Spelling would follow reading so that the words were spelled in context. Conversation was important to development of language in her classroom; Peabody would introduce questions of a philosophical nature to stimulate interest. She felt that studying language "touches into life the whole spiritual nature" (Marhshall, p. 108). Marshall (2005) describes how she taught mathematics:

> Children, she believed, could "discover and make the rules of arithmetic" on their own and understand them better in the process. Her students

worked with piles of dried beans, adding, subtracting, multiplying and diving them until they had master all the mathematical functions. (A similar system, using plastic chips, is now widely used in American grade schools) (p. 108)

Marhsall (2005) states that at that time it was in women's education that real innovations took place since boys' schools mostly involved "rote learning, competition for class rank, and corporal punishment" (p. 109). Elizabeth believed that the "mind has no sex" (p. 129) and that women were actually freer to engage more deeply into philosophical and spiritual issues.

After teaching in Maine for 2 years, Elizabeth and Mary opened a school in Brookline, Massachusetts. Elizabeth integrated the teachings from Channing into her school. She combined a rigorous intellectual curriculum with an emphasis on character development. At the end of the year she wrote each student a letter describing how they needed to improve in their behavior. Marshall notes that when the school opened again Elizabeth was "thrilled to discover that her letters had actually succeeded" (p. 154). Student behavior improved and one student who had been particularly difficult apologized for her behavior. Elizabeth also began Saturday morning classes for "older young ladies" that focused on religious and spiritual issues. Her aim was to awaken their inner wisdom. Of course, the notion that children had this inner wisdom ran counter to the view of children as basically sinful. One member of the Brookline community, Lewis Tappan, strongly disagreed with Peabody's approach and believed only parents should educate their children in the area of religion and spirituality. He wrote a harsh letter that questioned Elizabeth's "honor and integrity." Another parent was also upset so Elizabeth and Mary were forced to move their school again, this time to Boston.

TEMPLE SCHOOL

Elizabeth with help from Mary was considering starting up a school in Boston when she ran into Bronson Alcott (she had met him 4 years previously), who also starting a new school. Both shared the same vision of children as well as a similar approach to pedagogy. Ronda (1999) writes, "Both were educational empiricists, grounding their teaching in experience, trying to give pupils as much firsthand engagement with the objects of study as they could" (p. 114). Elizabeth began to approach families to see if they were interested in coming to the school. She also enlisted Channing's help and when the school started there were 25 students. The school is described in more detail in Chapter 3.

Peabody taught Latin and geography to the older students. She described her work in the school in a letter to a friend:

> What Mr Rodman calls the steam-engine system with children is entirely laid aside in this school—it is his object to cultivate the heart, and to bring out from the child's own mind the principles which are to govern his character. The outward manifestation of learning is not great, therefore, but the self-control that children exercise is of the first importance, and a foundation for all future good. I am reading Columbus to them, and able to give life to it by talking of the W. Indies from my own experience, which delights them very much. (Ronda, p. 120)

Elizabeth was also corresponding with Emerson during this period. They had met before when he was student at Harvard and he had tutored her in Greek. Now she sent him the manuscript of *Record of a School* and he responded with positive feedback. When the book was published, he wrote her that the book gave him "pleasure and hope."

As noted in the chapter on Alcott, Peabody became concerned about his book that recorded conversations with the children. There was also a disagreement with Alcott's wife. She was staying in the Alcott home and Abba Alcott read some of Elizabeth's letters to her sister, Mary. Upset by this invasion of privacy and increasingly concerned about the direction of the school, she moved out of the Alcott home and stopped working at the school.

Despite this difficult parting, her *Record of a School* describes one of the first holistic schools in North America and is one of the classic efforts in progressive education.

THE BOOKSTORE

Following the Temple School experience, Elizabeth found that parents were skeptical of experimental approaches to education so she turned to other activities. She edited a journal entitled *The Family School*. Ronda notes that the journal stayed away for progressive education and focused on more conventional stories of "duty, piety, and obedience" (p. 141).

Elizabeth and her sister, Sophia, met Nathaniel Hawthorne. Elizabeth was attracted to Hawthorne and tried to promote his work. She wrote a review of his *Twice-Told Tales* in the *New Yorker* and published other works of Hawthorne through the store. She was probably in love with Hawthorne, but he was much more attracted to Sophia and they eventually married.

Elizabeth also met Margaret Fuller. The two did not get along although they shared some similarities including the fact both were single women who did much to promote the status of women educationally. Ronda (1999) describes some of the differences.

Fuller was the more original thinker. In her views of gendered relations and particularly in her understanding of androgyny, in her critiques of American writing, and in her own often-brilliant journalism, Fuller shaped new paradigms still relevant today. One her side, Peabody was a much more pragmatic and synthetic thinker. She combined ideas, tried things out, and sought to build intellectual alliances, as in her effort to lessen the gap between Emerson and his Unitarian critics. (p. 158)

In July 1940, Elizabeth opened a bookstore and lending library on West Street in Boston. She specialized in foreign books that were not available elsewhere so that the shop attracted a number of intellectuals. One visitor called it a "Transcendental Exchange" where people not only bought books but met and discussed ideas. Ronda notes, "At West Street, people, ideas, and texts moved and merged" (p. 186). It was also the place where Fuller held her first conversations for women and the Ripleys met with people interested in their communal experiment that became Brook Farm. Peabody was an active participant in Fuller's conversations and was sympathetic to the Ripley's efforts. She saw Brook Farm as an educational experiment and referred to it as an "embryo University" (Ronda, p. 197). Her bookstore carried the first edition of *The Dial*, the transcendentalist journal, and it was where the final meeting of the Transcendental Club was held.

One person who encouraged her to start the store was Theodore Parker, the Unitarian minister who was to become a close intellectual companion of Peabody. Marshall (2005) notes that they were both "equally energetic, idealistic and impulsive" (p. 411). When Parker came to the bookstore, she would give him ideas for his sermons while he called her the "Boswell" of transcendentalism. He once wrote to her that "How wise must that heart be which can contain so many in its hold, and how deep its spiritual spring when they can all drink, and be satisfied" (Marshall, p. 412). Parker challenged Unitarian Orthodoxy and was shunned by his peers but he ended giving sermons at Boston's Music Hall, which were attended by huge audiences. Peabody called him the "son of Thunder."

During this period of the early 1840s Peabody was also writing. Ronda in his biography notes that Elizabeth was becoming more confident in her views and less concerned about propriety. One essay, "The Dorian Measure, with a Modern Application," argued for inclusion of the arts in the education of the whole child. She questioned spending so much money on the Mexican War when instead it could be spent on public education.

HISTORY IN THE CURRICULUM

Peabody saw history as a progression as humanity became more civilized and creative; for her history was the unfolding of a divine plan. She felt history should hold a major place in the curriculum so that children could see this unfolding. To assist in this process she was taken with the work of the Polish educator, Josef Bem. He developed a system of charts that for Peabody made the development of civilization clear and interesting to children. The charts also showed "that Herodotus was a contemporary of Nehemiah" so students could see across different civilizations and make connections. During the early part of the 1850s Elizabeth traveled throughout the east and part of the Midwest to promote Bem's work. Despite her enthusiasm, Bem's work was not appealing to most teachers as it required a heavy investment in materials that most school districts could not afford. Yet, her travels and extensive contacts that she made during this period provided the groundwork for her later work in promoting kindergarten which was much more successful.

In 1855, Elizabeth received some very positive news. A former student from the 1830s, Sarah Clarke, wrote that she was to receive a stipend of $100 a year because several former students had contributed to fund that provided financial support for Elizabeth. Clark wrote in her letter "Last year, some of your friends who love you and who think that you have spent your life and strength in working for others' benefit collected a sum of money and confided it to my brother William through me to invest for your use" (Ronda, p. 254). Not only was this income important to Elizabeth, but it was a testament to the work she had been doing for so many years.

KINDERGARTEN

During the 1840s and 50s Elizabeth had supported a number of reform movements including the anti-slavery and women rights movement. She also attended to the needs of her family, sometimes becoming an irritant to her sisters when Elizabeth commented on their child rearing practices. In 1860, however, Mary's husband Horace Mann, who brought educational reform to Massachusetts, died. His death brought Mary and Elizabeth together again. Mary invited Elizabeth to live with her and they began to collaborate on educational activities. Elizabeth became interested in the work of the German educator, Friedrich Froebel, who had developed a unique approach to educating young children that became the kindergarten. He believed that play and being in nature were important to the growth of young children.

In 1860, Elizabeth opened the first English speaking kindergarten in the United States in Boston's Beacon Hill district. In the following year, she had 30 students and was assisted by four adults. Her sister sometimes assisted as well; Mary believed the purpose of kindergarten was to bring forth the *soul* which was the "germ of everything" and nurturing the soul was true education. For both sisters, nurturing the soul was much more important than the emphasis then of keeping children quiet or focusing on "tangible" results.

Elizabeth wrote a booklet entitled *Moral Culture of Infancy and Kindergarten Guide* where she wrote about the importance of physical play and "Romping, the ecstasy of the body" (Ronda, p. 292). To learn more about Froebel's approach she went to Europe. There she met Emma Marwedel who would come to the United States to promote Froebel's work at every level of education. It was Marwedel who inspired Peabody to devote the rest of her life "to extend kindergarten over my own country" (Ronda, p. 299).

Her trip to Europe led her to revise the *Kindergarten Guide* and advocate that reading should not be in the kindergarten curriculum. This admonition came not only from talking to Froebel's followers but her own experience of trying to teach reading to children below the ages of six or seven where she witnessed "the painful effort of the brain"(Ronda, p. 304). She argued that kindergarten should rely on the arts and nature as the source of play. The teacher was not passive in this process but supported the play with the appropriate materials and attention to the individual child. Peabody's work was recognized by the United States Commissioner of Education, who consulted her about kindergarten. The United States Senate published 20,000 copies of her report on kindergarten. She also edited a journal, *Kindergarten Messenger,* which eventually was renamed the *Kindergarten Messenger and the New Education,* the journal of the American Froebel Union. The house in Boston where Elizabeth and Mary lived became a destination for those interested in the kindergarten movement.

Ronda argues that Peabody had such a strong impact because she was able to synthesize various elements into a vision of kindergarten that appealed to diverse groups. Her emphasis on play appealed to the progressive educators while her stress on play that was supervised and collective was attractive to more conservative parents (p. 308). She saw the importance of the socializing aspect of education as kindergarten "immersed children into the stream of society and history" (p. 309).

The last major project of Elizabeth's life was support of a school for the Paiutes Indians being proposed by Sarah Winnemucca. The Paiutes lived in Northern Nevada and southeastern Oregon. Elizabeth met Sarah when she came to Boston to talk about the need for a school for her people. Elizabeth and her friends were able to raise materials and cash for the school totaling almost $1,000. Sarah appreciated Elizabeth's help so much that she called it "The Peabody Indian School." The school took a bilingual approach to education, a real innovation at that time. Peabody wrote a booklet that advocated a multicultural and bilingual approach to education and argued against residential schools that took students away from their homes.

Elizabeth died in 1894 and she had become public figure by the time of her death. Ronda writes;

Peabody was symbol of dying to self and living for others. For a new generation of reformers coming of age at the turn of the century, who like Jane Addams felt sickened at the gap between the comfort of their lives and the poverty that surrounded them, Peabody was among the models whom they emulated. (p. 336)

PEABODY'S CONTRIBUTIONS TO EDUCATOIN

Kindergarten

Elizabeth Peabody's most lasting contribution was her advocacy for kindergarten, and particularly, a kindergarten that focused on physical activity, play and social interaction. Today, as we hear the call for more academic work in kindergarten, Peabody's vision of kindergarten is particularly relevant. Like Rudolf Steiner, Peabody believed that reading should not be taught in kindergarten; and like Steiner, she believed that sense experiences and physical activity provide the necessary ground for later academic work.

Vision of Child Development

Elizabeth Peabody had a clear vision of how children developed. It was not as detailed as ones that were later provided by Piaget and other developmental psychologists but she saw broad stages of development and suggested teaching strategies that were appropriate for each stage. The vision of the child development is one of a natural unfolding with gentle guidance from the teacher. She (1841) writes:

> This is all I shall do; I will not control, and tutor, and dictate, but keep away all that is harmful, supply ample nutriment to heart, intellect and the organs, and let them unfold in their own lovely proportions. I do not expect, by doing so much for them to obviate the necessity of self-education. I mean only to carry them as far as another can; and from this vantage-ground must begin self-education; which along secures peace and strength. (p. 8)

She describes her broad vision of child development in her book *Theory of Teaching*.

> In the child, we find immense physical and intellectual activity, extreme quickness of the senses, and susceptibility to impressions; a vivid conceptive faculty, and a flood of affection, bathing indiscriminately all which it approaches. We find a want of persistence in all its powers, bringing upon it often the reproach of volatility, which is really the mode in which Nature accomplishes the vast work of these early years, without fatiguing any part....

In youth, all the powers become discriminating. Where they attach themselves, it is with a stronger grasp. But they lose, partly, their instinctive character, and more guided by the apparent *worth* of things. Affection becomes feeling, and general activity is exchanged for enthusiasm for chosen pursuits, and in these there is generally no want of persistency. Still the powers have not reached full strength. They sometime break down; and the feelings alternate from the wildest hope to blank depression. (pp. 53–54)

In the early years, Peabody advocated experiences that heightened the children's senses. It was important for children to interact with concrete objects, and as mentioned above, she taught mathematics through concrete materials. She also encouraged children's direct experience with nature.

Role of the Teacher

This view of child development means that the teacher needs to be aware of the changing needs of the child. She (1841) writes that, "A teacher must also possess tact, a quick eye for the right moment to impart knowledge, to praise and to chide. She should have the habit of observing physical circumstances. Physical laws are paramount with children; hunger, thirst, sleep, are on them irresistible claims; it only when we have more to set against them, that we can ward them off for a time" (p. 67). For Peabody the teacher is constantly aware of the changing needs of the child.

Like Alcott and Emerson, Peabody believed in the importance of presence. She (1841) wrote "The difference between the living teacher and the dead book, cannot be set forth on paper; it must be felt to be appreciated" (p. 96). This was particularly important with regard to spiritual growth which "escapes analysis" and "is developed by a process too subtle for our perceptions" (p. 96).

Whole Child Education

Over the course of her career Peabody consistently argued for a holistic approach to education that focused body, mind, and soul. I mentioned above how she felt physical play was so important in kindergarten that wrote about "Romping, the ecstasy of the body." There was also a strong intellectual component to her work in elementary schools where history was a central component of the curriculum. In her book *Theory of Teaching with a Few Practical Illustrations*, she outlines very specifically how reading, spelling, grammar, mathematics, geography, French, and natural history can be taught.

Educating the moral and spiritual development of children was central to her vision of education. Peabody believed that nurturing the soul's development was fundamental to education. Through this process children see their place in the universe which involves moving beyond our egoism and seeing the "part … for which the human race was born" (p. 45). However, Peabody (1841) suggests that the teacher can "never exercise a direct influence on the soul" (p. 67). Nurturing the soul is done indirectly through the surrounding environment and through what Emerson called "the methods of love."

Happiness as a Goal of Education

Peabody wrote this in *Record of a School*:

> The realization of Happiness, involves the second principle of education; for it promotes the action of Love. When we lead a child to see the happiness within and around him, we are giving him a true perception of our love and leading himself through an experience of it. (p. 183)

The goal of happiness has been echoed in the work of Nel Noddings (2003) who has argued that happiness should be a central goal of education. Happiness is one of the main goals of the education system in Bhutan. Recently, that country invited 24 educators from around the world to align their education system with the country's goal of Gross National Happiness (Miller 2010).

Making Connections

Central to Elizabeth's pedagogy was making connections. In a letter to William T. Harris she (1984) wrote, "there is no *development* in the mind made by detached information—but things must be taught in *connections*." (p. 359). In her book on the theory of teaching she wrote (1841). "You will see that I aim at this in all my teachings; to give to each objects its widest significance, to connect it with many and high associations. This is the way to enlarge life and make it rich" (p. 56). One way that she did this was connecting subject material to individuals. She wrote, "Did you never observe how much more interesting facts become, when warmed by connexion with a person, or illuminated and their worth shown by a general law."(p. 52) She delighted in telling stories about people to show the human element in what the students were studying. This was one of the reasons that she felt history could be a central organizer of the curriculum because it allowed learning to be done in context. In her teaching, Elizabeth tried to set everything in context. In language study, she would first use words in sentences before they were studied (p. 78). She was constantly explaining why the students were studying a particularly topic and relating it to other elements in the curriculum. As mentioned earlier, geography and history were often connected.

Today making connections is central to holistic learning and to seeing the interdependence of things (Miller, 2007). Elizabeth was clearly a holistic educator and offers another transcendental model of holistic teaching and learning.

"Observe, Reflect, and Apply"

Observation and reflection were central to Elizabeth's pedagogy. She (1841) wrote, "teach them to observe, to reflect, to apply, to persevere; in short, to live earnestly, and according to intellectual laws; and they will be prepared for all we set before them"(p. 26). Observation and reflection were important both for teacher and student. It was never enough just to impart information but to observe, reflect on and apply the information.

Multicultural and Bilingual Education

With her work for the Paiutes School, Elizabeth became an advocate for bilingual and multicultural education. She was almost a century ahead of her time in this regard as multicultural education and bilingual education did not come into the mainstream till the 1960s. Governments should have listened to her critique of residential schools where native children were to experience various forms of abuse in Canada and the United States.

CONCLUSION

Of all the transcendentalists Alcott and Peabody were the most dedicated to education. As Ronda suggests, Peabody was the "practical intellectual" who was able to synthesize and thus had the most impact on educational practice. Unlike Alcott, she was able to read the social landscape and see what is possible. Her success with regard to Kindergarten was evidence of this.

In the epilogue to his biography of Peabody, Ronda describes how a "settlement house" was opened in her memory in Boston. Now called the Elizabeth Peabody House it moved to Summerville where is located in an old church building. It is now in ethnically diverse community including African American, Caribbean, Russian and middle-eastern cultures. There is a day care in the basement where children from these communities play and on the main floor where theater groups sometimes perform there is "a faded portrait of Elizabeth Peabody ... looking out over the fruit of her work" (p. 344).

REFERENCES

Channing, W. E. (2006). Humanity's likeness to God (1828). In L. Buell (Ed.), *The American transcendentalists: Essential writings* (pp. 11–15). New York, NY: Penguin.

Marshall, M. (2005). *The Peabody sisters: Three women who ignited American romanticism*. Boston: Houghton Mifflin.

Miller, J. (2007). *The holistic curriculum*. Toronto: University of Toronto Press.

Miller, J. (2010). Education for gross national happiness. *Encounter*. Spring 23. 231Web.htm.

Noddings, N. (2003). *Happiness and education*. Cambridge: Cambridge University Press.

Peabody, E. P. (1845). *The Record of a school. Exemplifying the general principles of spiritual culture*. Bedford, MA: Applewood Books.

Peabody, E. P. (1841). *Theory of teaching, with a few practical illustrations*. Boston. E. P. Peabody.

Peabody, E. P. (1984). *Letters of Elizabeth Palmer Peabody: American renaissance woman*. B. A. Ronda (Ed.). Middletown, CN: Wesleyan University Press.

Ronda, B. A. (1999). *Elizabeth Palmer Peabody: A reformer on her own terms*. Cambridge, MA: Harvard University Press.

CHAPTER 7

A TRANSCENDENTAL PEDAGOGY

"That which we are, we shall teach"

—Emerson

Most educational approaches have a theoretical basis (explicit or implicit) and a set of teaching strategies used in the classroom. A third factor is that the approach comes through the being, or presence of the teacher. In this chapter, I will attempt to present how these three aspects were manifested in the work of the Transcendentalists and thus form the core of a transcendental pedagogy.

THEORY: THE PERENNIAL PHILOSOPHY

The underlying principles of transcendental learning are closely linked to what has been called the Perennial Philosophy. The search for the perennial philosophy can be traced to thinkers such as Plotinus and Augustine. The term was first used by Agostino Steuco in referring the work of the Renaissance philosopher, Marsilio Ficino. Leibniz picked up this thread in 18th century. In the last century Aldous Huxley (1970) wrote a book on this topic and today Ken Wilber (1997) has articulated his vision of the perennial philosophy. Jorge Ferrer (2002) has developed a revisionist version that he calls a "Relaxed Universalism" which addresses the concern of not

Trancendental Learning: The Educational Legacy of Alcott, Emerson,
Fuller, Peabody and Thoreau, pp. 89–104
Copyright © 2011 by Information Age Publishing

properly acknowledging diversity within perennialism. Below are some basic principles of the perennial philosophy as articulated by Emerson and Thoreau.

Unity/Diversity

At the risk of reductionism, the simplest expression of the perennial philosophy is Bono's statement "We are one, but not the same"; in other words, we are all part of whole yet within that whole lies great diversity. The perennial philosophy acknowledges diversity and that the universe is in process; however, underlying the diversity and change is a unity. This unity, however, is not monistic; instead, the emphasis is on the relationships between the whole and the part, or the one and the many. In fact, it is this relationship that is at the heart of the perennial philosophy. Ferrer refers to Martin Buber (1970) and Mendes-Flohr (1989) and the realm of "the Between" which is the place between objects. Also this "in between" is not static but dynamic. David Bohm (1980) referred to this as holomovement and he stated that "holomovement is undefinable and immeasurable" (p. 151).

In *Nature* Emerson (2003) writes of Unity and diversity:

> So intimate is this Unity, that, it is easily seen, it lies under the undermost garment of nature, and betrays its source in Universal Spirit. For it pervades Thought also. Every universal truth which we express in words implies or supposes every other truth.... It is like great circle on a sphere, comprising all possible circles; which however, may be drawn, and comprise it, in like manner. Every such truth is the absolute Ens seen from one side. But it has innumerable sides. (p. 205)

"Innumerable sides" catches the nature of diversity in the Unity that Emerson so beautifully describes.

Thoreau also saw the interrelatedness of things and Robinson (2004) summarizes this perspective when he writes that Thoreau's "growing belief that the study of nature was the recognition of an ever-enlarging network of relations, in which natural objects were defined through their part in a larger system, and thus through the process of their interactions" (p. 184). As noted in the chapter on Thoreau, he actually used the phrase the "perennial mind" which refers to an inherent wisdom within each person.

For education, this principle suggests that the curriculum should focus on connections at every level, which will be discussed in the last chapter (Miller, 2007; Miller, 2010). If there is this unity or interconnectedness at all levels of the universe then a curriculum that is fragmented and unconnected is simply out of touch with how things are. Unfortunately, most curricula are divided into courses, units and lessons with little effort to connect all this information.

Emerson wrote that the child gradually begins to discover the "roots running underground, whereby contrary and remote things cohere, and flower out from one stem" (p. 228). Transcendental learning should facilitate this process by developing a curriculum of connectedness. This is the focus of the last chapter.

Macrocosm/Microcosm

Another facet of this perennial philosophy is that each part of the universe represents the whole. Emerson (2003) wrote: "A leaf, a drop, a crystal, a moment of time is related to the whole, and partakes of the perfection of the whole. Each particle is a microcosm, and faithfully renders the likeness of the world" (p. 204). Most important for the Transcendentalists was the idea that within each person lies a spark that is actually a microcosm of the Whole. In his lecture on The American Scholar, Emerson wrote "in yourself is the law of all nature" (p. 244). Emerson wrote in his journal "In all my lectures, I have taught one doctrine, namely, the infinitude of the private man" (p. 65). This infinitude is similar to what David Marshak (1997) calls the *inner teacher* as he suggests that holistic educators in the twentieth century, such as Rudolf Steiner, also believed in nourishing the soul life of children to awaken the *inner teacher*. Marshak writes:

> In particular, helping the child's and youth's spiritual being to unfold, so that it can manifest as her *inner teacher* and express its innate wisdom for guiding her growth; helping the child and youth to follow the calling of her *inner teacher* within her spiritual being, which will lead her to meet her developmental needs. (p. 19)

This idea was central to the Transcendentalist's view of education as the role of the teacher was to nourish this inner teacher, the soul. As we saw in the chapter on Alcott, his conversations with the students were aimed at drawing out the inherent wisdom of the child.

Contemplation

One way to see the interconnectedness of things is through contemplation. In contrast to analysis, which breaks things into parts, contemplation allows us to see the Whole and the relationship of the part to the Whole. Emerson (2003) wrote about contemplation in his journal:

> In the history of the intellect no more important fact than the Hindu theology, teaching that the beatitude or supreme good is to be attained through science; namely, by the perception of the real and unreal, setting aside matter,

and qualities, and affections or emotions and persons, and actions, as Maias or illusions, and thus arriving at the *contemplation* (my italics) of the one eternal Life & Cause. (p. 171)

Thoreau (1986) in *Walden* also called for a contemplative approach to life.

When we are unhurried and wise, we perceive that only great and worthy things have any permanent and absolute existence—that petty fears and petty pleasures are but the shadow of the reality. This is always exhilarating and sublime. (p.140)

Emerson (1966) believed that children in school should have the opportunity to contemplate.

The solitary knows the essence of thought, the scholar in society only its fair face. There is now want of example of great men, great benefactors, who have been monks and hermits in habit.... Let him study the art of solitude, yield as gracefully as he can to his destiny. (p. 216)

The Transcendentalists also believed in learning by doing and working with one's hands but nourishing contemplation was also fundamental to their view of education. I have argued in the other contexts that education today continues to ignore this mode of knowing and should be integrated into the curriculum to create a more holistic education (Miller, 1994; Miller, 2006).

Compassionate Action

If we are connected to each other, then ultimately we feel the need to guide our actions through this understanding. The experience of interconnectedness lets us see ourselves in others and through this process a natural compassion arises. There were a range of perspectives with regard to this aspect of the perennial philosophy among the Transcendentalists. Emerson and Thoreau were both against slavery and supported abolition through various measures. As mentioned in the first chapter they planted the seed of nonviolence that grew with Tolstoy, Gandhi, and King. Orestes Brownson and Theodore Parker were more radical in their call for social reform. Parker at the beginning of his career as a Unitarian minister agreed with Browson's ideas on social reform; however, in his later years, he devoted almost all of his energy to the abolition movement.

Brownson was the most radical as he argued for the abolition of hereditary property.

He rejected the focus on the "self" and called for Christians to change society:

> To bring down the high, and bring up the low; to break the fetters of the bound and set the captive free; to destroy all oppression, establish the reign of justice, which is the reign of equality, between man and man; to introduce new heaven and a new earth, where dwelleth righteousness, wherein all shall be as brothers loving one another, and non one possessing what another lacketh. (Gura, p. 139)

Although the Transcendentalists differed regarding their approach to compassionate action, they were all critical of exploitive institutions, particularly slavery.

PRACTICES: AIMS AND GOALS

One of the ultimate goals of transcendental learning is *self-knowledge*. In *The Record of the School* Peabody (1845) writes that Alcott "was glad to hear that one of the scholars had said out of school, that it was impossible to remain in Mr Alcott's school and not learn to know one's self" (p. 85). Since the self was closely connected to the soul for the transcendentalists the development of the soul was also a goal. Again Peabody (1845) quotes Alcott:

> We need schools not for the inculcation of knowledge, merely, but the development of genius. Genius is the peculiar attribute of the soul. It is the soul, indeed, in full and harmonious play; and no instruction deserves the name, that does not quicken this essential life, and fit it for representation in literature, art or philosophy. (p. 17)

Peabody (1845) argues that teachers and parents must also embark on the path of self-knowledge if the students are to know themselves. "The parent or teacher should make it his first business to know himself; for most surely he will transmit his moral character by inspiration to his child in just such proportion as circumstances allow to have any influence, and the child has any sensibility" (p. 187).

Another goal was *happiness*. Peabody writes:

> The realization of Happiness, involves the second principle of education; for it promotes the action of Love. When we lead a child to see the happiness within and around him, we are giving him a true perception of our love and leading himself through an experience of it. (p. 183)

This happiness can come also from being in nature and beholding its wonders. Emerson (2003) writes about the poet but it could also apply to the student:

> So the poet's habit of living should be set on a key so low, that common influences should delight him. His cheerfulness should be the gift of sunlight; the air should suffice for his inspiration, and he should be tipsy with water. That spirit which suffices quiet hearts, which seems to come forth to such from every dry knoll of sere grass, from every pine stump and half-imbedded stone, on which the dull March sun shines comes forth to the poor and hungry, and such as are of simple taste. (p. 341)

It was Thoreau (2002) who said "Surely joy is the condition of life." (p. 5) Thoreau (1999) also called for us to find joy in the simple pleasures of daily life. "I wish to live ever as to derive my satisfactions and inspirations from the commonest events, every-day phenomena, so that what my senses hourly perceive, my daily walk, the conversation of my neighbors, may inspire me, and I may dream of no heaven but that which lives about me." (p. 42). Emerson (2003) believed that seeing the miraculous is an "invariable mark of wisdom." (p. 223)

Wisdom is another major goal of transcendental learning. Thoreau (1999) argued that "Wisdom is the result of education, and education being the bringing out, or development, of that which is in a man, by contact with the Not Me, is safer in the hands of Nature than of Art" (p. 53). The "Not Me" that Thoreau referring to is the Self rather than the ego or the little self. Thoreau (2002) also claims that "Wisdom does not inspect, but behold" (p. 23). He adds that we learn not by "inference and deduction" but by "direct intercourse and sympathy" (p. 23). Wisdom then does not come from analysis but from direct experience and our empathic imagination.

Finally, another major aim of transcendental learning is *connection* to the earth, it's processes and the cosmos. Emerson asked "Why should not we also enjoy an original relation to the universe?" Thoreau (1961) also described this desire when he wrote:

> My desire for knowledge is intermittent but my desire to commune with the spirit of the universe, to be intoxicated even with the fumes, call it, of that divine nectar, to bear my head through atmospheres and over heights unknown to my feet, is perennial & constant. (pp. 41–42)

As noted above, Thoreau also sought this connection in the simple acts of daily life. The connection to nature also facilitates self-knowledge. Emerson (2003) wrote: "And, in fine, the ancient precept, "Know thyself," and the modern precept, "Study nature," become at last one maxim" (p. 228) Studying nature students see that they are part of nature which is "intricate, overlapped, interweaved, and endless." (p. 433)

PRINCIPLES OF LEARNING

The Transcendentalist saw learning as organic and rejected mechanistic approaches to teaching. Emerson wrote (2003) in his journal that "We are shut up in schools and college recitation rooms for 10 or 15 years and come out at last with a bellyful of words and do not know a thing. We cannot use our hands or our legs or our eyes or our arms" (p. 60). Below are some of the key principles of learning, which were identified by the transcendentalists.

Holistic Perspective/Educating the Whole Person

Elizabeth Peabody and Margaret Fuller advocated holistic view of the individual. Fuller used the symbolism of Minerva and the Muse as archetypes for the integration of women (Chapter 4, "Holistic Perpsective") Throughout her career Peabody also advocated an education that found a balance between the mental, physical and spiritual. Ignoring any of these elements was very problematic since she saw them as deeply interconnected in the human being.

Experiential Learning

Thoreau (2002) states that wisdom arises through "direct intercourse and sympathy" with nature. (p. 23) He wrote, "The true man of science will know nature better by his finer organization; he will smell, taste, see, hear, feel, better than other men. His will be a deeper and finer experience" (pp. 22–23). Alcott also believed in the importance of experience. In the appendix of *Record of a School* there are letters from students and one wrote to Alcott, "Experience is as much our teachers as you are; you teach us how to learn from her" (p. 208).

Using All the Senses

Alcott believed that learning to read and write was facilitated by having children have direct sense experiences. He felt that sight was particularly important and he showed pictures of words and encouraged the students to draw. Peabody (1845) describes the importance of drawing and writing at a very early age. "To aid the practice of the eye, in looking at forms, the practice of the hand in imitating them should soon follow. Mr Alcott thinks the slate and pencil, or the chalk and black board, can hardly be given too early. The latter is even better than the former; for children should have free scope, as we find that their first shapings are almost gigantic" (p. 5).

The process that Alcott used in teaching reading and writing will be described in more detail in the next section.

Thoreau, of course, encouraged his student to see, smell, and touch what they were studying. This leads us to the next principle of embodiment.

Embodiment

Learning should embrace the whole person—hands, head and heart. Thoreau (1961) believed that "We reason from our hands to our head." (p. 57) For Emerson (2003) living was the ultimate teacher. "Only so much do I know, as I have lived.... Life is our dictionary. Years are well spent in country labors; in town—in the insight into men and women; in science; in art; to the one end of mastering in all their facts a language by which to illustrate and embody our perceptions." (pp. 233–235) Thoreau went to Walden so that he reduce life to its most basic terms. In his eulogy on Thoreau, Emerson (2003) commented on how Thoreau's walking was the source of his writing.

> He was a good swimmer, runner, skater, boatman, and would probably out-walk most countrymen in a day's journey. And the relation of body to mind was till finer than we have indicated.... The length of his walk uniformly made the length of his writing. If shut up in the house, he did not write at all. (p. 460)

Emerson also liked to walk in countryside around Concord and then would return to his study and enter his reflections in his journal that he kept in a round table. These reflections eventually evolved into his lectures and essays.

Nourishing the Inner Life and the Imagination

The Transcendentalists want to nourish the inner life of the student. Emerson (1990) wrote; "Colleges can only highly serve us when they aim not to drill, but to create; when they gather from every ray of various genius to their hospitable halls, and by the concentrated fires set the hearts of their youth on flame." (p. 88) Peabody (1845) in commenting on Alcott's teaching of geography wrote: "For it is a fact, which every thoughtful teacher must have observed, that nothing is permanently remembered, which does not touch the heart, or interest the imagination" (pp. 124–125).

Emerson also believed in the "remedial forces of the soul" in the child, which can be nourished through patience. I think Emerson would like Parker Palmer's (1999) definition of the soul:

As we proceed, let us remember one thing about the human soul: it is like a wild animal. It is tough, self-sufficient, resilient, and exceedingly shy. If we go crashing through the woods, screaming and yelling for the soul to come out, it will evade us all day and night. We cannot beat the bushes and yell at each other and expect this precious inwardness to emerge. But if we are willing to go into the woods and sit quietly at the base of a tree, this wild thing will, after a few hours, reveal itself. Out of the corner of our eye, we might glimpse something of the wild preciousness we all are looking for. (p. 16)

In teaching we do not approach the soul directly but instead create conditions that are supportive of the soul's growth. Thus, we might "glimpse something of wild preciousness."

Balance in the Curriculum

Although the Transcendentalists believed in experiential learning and nourishing the imagination, they did not dismiss traditional approaches to learning. Emerson (1966) spoke to teachers and said:

Nor are the two elements, enthusiasm and drill, incompatible. Accuracy is essential to beauty. The very definition of the intellect is Aristotle's: "that by which we know terms or boundaries." Give a boy accurate perceptions. Teach him the difference between the similar and the same. Make him call things by their right names. Pardon in him no blunder. (p. 219)

Thoreau studied the classics and referred to them throughout *Walden*. He could read them in the original Latin or Greek.

Community-Based Learning

The community of Concord was important to Transcendentalists, particularly Alcott, Emerson, and Thoreau. During his life, Alcott was always looking to return to Concord when he was living in Boston or elsewhere.... The community was equally important to Thoreau and Emerson so the concept of community-based learning was also significant. Thoreau (1999) wrote:

As some give to Harvard College or another institution, why might not another give a forest or huckleberry field to Concord? A town is an institution which deserves to be remembered. We boast of our system of education, but why stop at schoolmasters and school houses? We are all schoolmasters, and our schoolhouse is the universe. To attend chiefly to the desk or schoolhouse while we neglect scenery in which it is placed is absurd. If we do not look out we shall find our fine schoolhouse standing in a cowyard at last. (pp. 45–46)

Alcott, when he was superintendent of schools for Concord, wanted Thoreau to write a textbook on the history and geography of Concord to be used in schools and to be supplemented by field trips. Unfortunately, Thoreau's illness and death prevented this project from being completed.

Life-Long Learning

Just as the Transcendentalists believed that education was not confined to the school house they also thought the learning was a life-long quest. Both Alcott and Fuller were adult educators. Their "conversations" engaged adults in range of issues and topics. Bickman (1999) also argues that Thoreau was "a pioneer in adult education through his work as both an organizer and a lecturer in the lyceum movement…. Thoreau was an advocate for *continuing* education more fundamentally in the sense that he knew that no formulation or system is sufficient or permanent, that to be responsively alive is to be a perpetual learner, always aware of both the possibilities and the limits of one's current knowledge." (p. xiv)

All the transcendentalists believed in the importance of individual reflection and keeping a journal throughout their lives.

Multicultural and Bilingual Education

With her work for the Paiutes School, Elizabeth Peabody became an advocate for bilingual and multicultural education. She was almost a century ahead of her time in this regard as multicultural education and bilingual education did not come into the mainstream till the 1960s. Governments should have listened to her critique of residential schools where native children were to experience various forms of abuse in Canada and the United States.

TEACHING STRATEGIES

Journal Writing

Just as the transcendentalists kept journals, they encouraged their students to do the same. At the Temple School the first task in the morning was for the students to write in their journals. Margaret Fuller also had her students write extensively in their journals when she was teaching school. The main object of the journal writing was the development of the student's soul life.

Autobiography/Biography

Closely connected to journal writing was narrative and autobiography. In the *Record of a School* Peabody writes about how Alcott saw autobiography as a way for the more mature student to reflect on the development of the soul (p. 193).

Regarding history, Emerson (2003) believed that we can learn much by studying the lives of individuals. He wrote: "All history becomes subjective; in other words, there is properly no history, only biography" (p. 54). Emerson wrote reflective essays on several individuals such as Napoleon, Montaigne, and Swedenborg. Study of biographies then would not just focus on the external events of a person's life but on their inward struggles such as Lincoln's melancholy.

Inquiry Based Learning

Alcott employed a form of Socratic questioning with the students. He rarely lectured to the students but led them through a series of questions.

Examples of some of these inquiries were presented in the chapter on Alcott. Peabody records many examples in *Record of a School*. Sometimes this would involve extended questioning of one pupil or just presenting a general question to the entire class such as "what is the imagination." (p. 165). Sometimes the questions were very leading so that Peabody (1845) once wrote that he "unconsciously led them to his views" (p. 158).

In her both teaching of young women and in conversations, Fuller engaged the students with challenging questions.

Classroom Circles

Alcott had the students sit in a semicircle rather than in rows which was very unusual for that time. The semicircle supported the discussion amongst the students since they could see each other's faces. The use of the circle as a vehicle for meeting and discussion can be traced back to indigenous peoples. For example, Emerson's essay on "Circles" confirms their importance in the universe as he wrote "the natural world may be conceived of as a system of concentric circles." (p. 320).

Nature-Based Learning

Both Emerson and Thoreau believed that learning should not be confined to the classroom. Thoreau, of course, was an advocate of taking students into the outdoors. It was there that he could encourage inquiry based on the environment (see Chapter 5 for examples). Thoreau has since inspired many outdoor and environmentally based educational programs.

Images/Visualization

Alcott used pictures and images to teach language. Peabody describes his approach in *Record of a School*.

> When children are committed to his charge very young the first discipline to which he puts them, is of the eye; by making them familiar with pictures. The art of drawing has been well called the art of learning to see.... It is from considerations of this kind that Mr Alcott very early presents to children pictured forms of things; and he selects them in the confidence that the general character of these forms will do much towards setting the direction of the current activity. (pp. 4–5)

The image can help the student develop their own inner images, which are important in the development of imagination. Steiner and other educators have argued that elementary school children need to develop their imagination and that stories, fairy tales and myths are helpful in this process because they trigger the inner life of the child.

PRESENCE OF THE TEACHER

Emerson (2003) once wrote, "That which we are, we shall teach" (p. 305). He recognized that the teacher's being and presence were at the center of the teaching/learning process. Alcott (1872) in talking about conducting his conversations also emphasized the importance of presence when he wrote, "We give what we are, not necessarily what we know; nothing more, nothing less, and only to our kind, those playing best their parts who have the nimblest wits, taking out the egotism, the nonsense; putting wisdom, information in their place." (p. 75).

How does one develop this presence? It comes through caring for the soul and contemplation. Walking in the woods, writing in the journals, reading the works of the ancients were ways that the Transcendentalists cultivated the soul. Thoreau describes a form of contemplation at Walden where he sat on the front steps of his cabin "rapt in revery."

Being in the present requires constant attention. This constant awareness was particularly stressed by the Stoics. Thoreau read the Stoics and might have agreed with Pierre Hadot (2002) who has argued how ancient philosophy was a form of contemplative practice. Hadot (2002) states: "To live in a philosophical way meant, above all, to turn toward intellectual and spiritual life, carrying out a conversion which involved "the whole soul"—which is to say the whole of moral life" (p. 65). Philosophy then could be called an education of the soul. Hadot describes various spiritual exercises that ancient philosophers pursued in their work; they practiced various forms of contemplation such as being fully present in the moment. For example, the Roman poet and philosopher, Horace wrote: "Let the soul be happy in the present, and refuse to worry about what will come later.... Think about arranging the present as best you can, with serene mind. All else is carried away as by a river." (Hadot, p. 196). Hadot suggests that the Stoics practiced their own form of being present.:

> For them, philosophy was a unique act which had to be practiced at each instant, with constantly renewed attention (*proshoke*) to oneself and to the present moment.... Thanks to this attention, the philosopher is always perfectly aware not only what he is doing, but also of what he is thinking (this is the task of lived logic) and of what he is—in other words, of his place within the cosmos. (p. 138)

Today, there has been extensive work in the area of mindfulness meditation which stresses the importance of being present and attentive to our immediate environment. (Schoeberlein, 2009). Mindfulness is a form of contemplation that can develop presence. In my work, I have introduced teachers to mindfulness practice as a way of enhancing their presence as teachers. (Miller, 2006). Below is how one elementary school teacher became more attentive to the needs of an individual student and the difference she felt this made. This student, ZR, had been acting out a great deal in the classroom.

> Today ZR and I spoke briefly about his difficulty to focus. Today was particularly difficult for him. He did try very hard. As other students responded during our math discussion, he wiggled and wiggled in his seat. In the past, I had been frustrated with him—his distractions became the class' distractions. Today, I was mindful. I only thought of him in that moment.
>
> I felt a great deal of empathy for him. I remembered how difficult it had been (and sometimes still is) for me to sit still in class. He looked at me watching him with what seemed like a slightly guilty look. I smiled at him and he smiled back and seemed to be trying even harder to sit still, to focus.
>
> After the discussion was over and the students worked on their project, I went over to talk with him. (He has chosen to sit by himself at desk right next to mine). We had good talk. I listened to his talk. Eventually, he suggested taking breaks between his work. He promised to work hard. I said we could try it for few days and then bring the suggestion to his parents as he also expressed concern about difficulties focusing during his homework.

Later this teacher and ZR met with his parents.

> ZR and I had a meeting with his parents after school today. We presented them with a simple "schedule" for his day—10 min of work followed by a 10 min break. I sensed by his mother's response that she was quite taken aback. This was school and he should be able to focus. His sister did her homework without any breaks. ZR explained, as much as he could, how and why he was having difficulty and why he felt the 10 min breaks might help. He promised to work very hard during the 10 min work-outs. Because he had actually been experimenting, I could vouch that he had been working very hard and producing excellent work.
>
> I think this meeting was the first that I have had in a long time where I felt that I was there. I was not worried about getting home. I was not concerned about what they would think of me as a teacher. My own experience with a "cluttered mind" made me believe that for ZR to be 'here; and present, he needed breaks to immerse himself in his art. I felt comfortable. We will monitor this strategy until the Christmas break and revisit in January.

In the day when drugs are administered to children so they can settle down, this example shows how this teacher's presence made a difference in this students' life.

CONCLUSION

Ultimately, transcendental pedagogy seeks soul-to-soul connection between teacher and student. Within each student is a mysterious destiny. Carl Jung said: "I simply believe that some part of the human Self or Soul is not subject to the laws of space and time."(cited in Winokur, 1990, p. 73) The teacher's simple awareness of this aspect of humanity can lead to true empowerment. We empower our students when we can acknowledge this aspect in their lives; if we do not then it may be not be released. In the Gnostic Gospels Jesus is quoted as saying: "If you bring forth what is within you, what you bring forth will save you. If you do not bring forth what is within you, what you do not bring forth will destroy you."(cited in Pagels, 1979, p. xv) If we are not sensitive to what is within the student it may not be brought forth. Emerson wrote about the student "It is chosen and foreordained, and he only holds the key to his own secret."(p. 217) Transcendental learning then attempts to connect with and nurture this part of the human being, which is so often neglected in our classrooms. The Transcendentalists focused on nourishment of the soul and have given us the blueprint for this important work.

Today Holistic education, which focuses on the development of the whole person—body, mind and soul, continues the legacy of the Transcendentalists. The next chapter explores how a Transcendentalist's pedagogy can be developed with in the current framework of holistic education.

REFERENCES

Alcott, A. B. (1872). *Concord Days*. Boston: Robert Brothers.

Bickman, M. (1999). "Introduction" in *Uncommon learning: Henry David Thoreau on education*. Boston: Houghton Mifflin. (pp. viii–xxxiiii)

Bohm, D. (1980). *Wholeness and the implicate order*. London: Routledge & Kegan Paul.

Buber, M. (1970). *I and thou*. (W. Kaufman, Trans.). New York: Scribner.

Emerson, R. W. (1966). *Emerson on education*. H. M. Jones (Ed.). New York: Teachers College Press.

Emerson, R. W. (1990). *Ralph Waldo Emerson: Selected essays, lectures and poems*. New York, NY: Bantam.

Emerson, R. W. (2003). *Selected writings of Ralph Waldo Emerson*. New York: Signet Classic.

Ferrer, J. N. (2002). *Revisioning transpersonal theory: A participatory vision of human spirituality*. Albany, NY: SUNY press.

Gura, P. F. (2007). *American transcendentalism: A history*. New York, NY: Hill and Wang.

Hadot, P. (2002). *What is ancient philosophy?* Cambridge, MA: Belknap Press.

Huxley, A. (1970). *The perennial philosophy*. New York, NY: Harper Colophon.

Marshak, D. (1997). *The common vision: Parenting and educating for wholeness*. New York, NY: Peter Lang.

Mendes-Flohr, P. (1989). *From mysticism to dialogue: Martin Buber's transformation of German social thought*. Detroit: Wayne State University Press.

Miller, J. P. (1994). *The contemplative practitioner: Meditation in education and the professions*. Westport, Connecticut: Bergin & Garvey.

———— (2006). *Educating for wisdom and compassion: Creating conditions for timeless learning*. Thousand Oaks, CA: Corwin.

———— (2007). *The holistic curriculum*. Toronto: University of Toronto Press.

———— (2010). *Whole child education*. Toronto: University of Toronto Press.

Pagels, E. (1979). *The gnostic gospels*. New York, NY: Vintage Books

Palmer, P. (1999). The grace of great things: Reclaiming the sacred in knowing, teaching and learning. In Glazer, S. (Ed.), *The heart of learning; Spirituality in education*. New York, NY: Tarcher/Putnam.

Peabody, E. (1845). *Record of a school*. Bedford, MA: Applewood Books.

Robinson, D. M. (2004). *Natural life: Thoreau's worldly transcendentalism*. Ithaca, NY: Cornell University Press.

Schoeberlein, D. (2009). *Mindful teaching and teaching mindfulness: A guide for anyone who teaches anything*. Boston: Wisdom publications.

Thoreau, H. D. (1961). *The heart of Thoreau's journals*. Shepard, O. (Ed.). New York, NY: Dover

Thoreau, H. D. (1986). *Walden and civil disobedience*. New York, NY: Penguin.

Thoreau, H. D. (1999). *Uncommon learning: Henry David Thoreau on education*. Bickman, M. (Ed.). Boston: Houghton Mifflin.

Thoreau, H. D. (2002). *The essays of Henry D. Thoreau*. Hyde, L. (Ed.). New York, NY: North Point Press.

Wilber, K. (1997). *The eye of the spirit: An integral vision for a world gone slightly mad*. Boston: Shambhala.

Winokur, J. (1990). *Zen to go*. New York, NY: Penguin Books.

CHAPTER 8

EDUCATIONAL LEGACY OF TRANSCENDENTALISM: HOLISTIC EDUCATION

When a man stupid becomes a man inspired. . . .No horizon shuts down. He sees things in their causes, all fact in their connection.

—Emerson

In a masterful analysis of Emerson's thought, Neal Dolan (2009) uses the word "holistic" to describe much of Emerson's work. For example, in writing about Emerson's chapter on "Beauty" in *Nature* he refers to Emerson's "broad holistic perspective that the essay attempts to inculcate." In referring to Emerson's *Representative Men,* Dolan writes,

> Indeed, in Emerson's account, each representative man attempts in distinctive ways to do exactly what Emerson seeks to do in his work as whole: to enfold the scientific-empirical world of infinitely multitudinous particulars into a comprehensive, holistic, interlocking and psychological resonant verbal-symbolic order. (p. 225)

I agree with this analysis and in this chapter, I argue that this holistic perspective underlies Transcendental pedagogy and is reflected today in what is called holistic education (Miller, 2007; Miller, 2010).

Trancendental Learning: The Educational Legacy of Alcott, Emerson, Fuller, Peabody and Thoreau, pp. 105–124

The term holistic education did not arise until the mid to late 1980s. It was at that time the *Holistic Education Review* was first published in 1988. In his book on holistic education Gallegos (2001) writes about the word holistic and its meaning:

> The term "holistic" comes from the Greek holos, which in our context means wholeness. The term refers to comprehending reality as a function of a whole in integrated processes. The term "holistic" is used to denote that reality is an undivided whole; that it is not fragmented; that the entirety is fundamental reality. The whole, from such a perspective, is not a static structure, but a universal, impermanent flow....The holistic vision is based on an integration of knowledge. Science, art, spirituality and traditions interface with one another to create a culture of wisdom that overcomes the fragmentation of knowledge manifested in the academic disciplines. Given that it is not possible to comprehend the new reality from isolated disciplines, however, the holistic vision is transdisciplinary in nature. (p.13)

Holistic education is based on this view of reality and attempts to integrate disciplines and perspectives so that student can see relationships and interconnectedness. Holistic educators also agree that education should focus on the whole person (e.g., head, hands, and heart). In my book, *The Holistic Curriculum*, I focus on six connections that encourage students to see relationships in this manner. The last three connections focus on the individual and first three center on the integrated learning, the earth and community.

The following are the six connections:

- Subject Connections
- Community Connections
- Earth Connections
- Thinking Connections
- Body-Mind Connections
- Soul Connections

In this chapter, I first identify what the Transcendentalists wrote about each connection and then explore the connection in the context of today's education and current curriculum practices.

SUBJECT CONNECTIONS

The Transcendentalists saw life as interconnected. In *Nature*, Emerson (2003) wrote that Idealism does not see things and events as separate but "as one vast picture." Emerson describes how gradually the young person begins to see the interconnectedness in this "vast picture":

> To the young mind, everything is individual, stands by itself. By and by it finds how to join things and see in them on nature; … it goes on tying things together, diminishing anomalies, discovering roots running underground which by contrary and remote things cohere and flower from one stem. (p. 227)

Holistic education facilitates connections between subjects so that the student may see what John Dewey called the unity of all knowledge. Connections among subjects is also referred to as integrated curriculum. This can occur on a number of levels. The first level is the *multidisciplinary*. Here, the curriculum retains separate subjects, but establishes linkages between the separate subjects. For example, the history teacher might reference the literature and art of a specific historical period and explore how the art was representative of that period. At the *interdisciplinary* level, two or three subjects are integrated around a theme or problem. For example, in examining the problem of city traffic and other problems of urban planning, subjects such as economics, political science, design technology and mathematics can be brought together and integrated. At the *transdisciplinary* level, several subjects are integrated around a broad theme. Issues such as poverty and violence in society lend themselves to this broadly integrative approach. At each level, connections between subjects and concepts become more numerous and complex.

James Beane (1997) is an advocate of interdisciplinary integrated curriculum. Beane believes that the curriculum should move away from fragmented approaches where knowledge is kept within the boundaries of separate subjects. For Beane, the central features of integrated curriculum include:

> First, the curriculum is organized around problems and issues that are of personal and social significance in the real world. Second, learning experiences in relation to the organizing center are planned so as to integrate pertinent knowledge in the context of the organizing centers. Third, knowledge is developed and used to address the organizing center currently under study rather than to prepare for some later test or grade level. Finally, emphasis is placed on substantive projects and other activities that involve real application of knowledge. (p. 9)

The final key feature of Beane's approach is the participation of students in curriculum planning. He suggests that students participate by identifying questions related to personal issues and those that are oriented towards society and culture. The former could include questions such as "What kind of job will I have when I become an adult?" and "Will I get married?" Societal oriented questions might include "Why do people hate each other?" and "Will racism ever end?" After all the questions have been put up on the board or chart paper, the teacher negotiates with the students—themes, or organizing centers, based on the questions. These themes are usually broad and include "conflict and violence," "living in the future" and "money." Beane suggests using a concept web with the central theme in the middle and with a number of sub-themes surrounding the main theme. The students research the theme and sub-themes and then can present their conclusions through some kind of activity or performance. For example, a class focusing on the environment decided to divide into five sub-groups to create five large scale biomes in their classroom. Another class working with the theme of living in the future developed a vision of what their city will be like in the year 2030.

Through these projects students see how knowledge and subjects are connected and related to problems in real life.

Another powerful framework for integrated curriculum comes from Susan Drake (1998, 2007). She argues that curriculum can be organized around three broad areas of Knowing, Doing, and Being with the last area being a place of exploring soul.

COMMUNITY CONNECTIONS

Community is essential to holistic education. Students should study and work in an environment of caring and love. Martin Luther King talked of the "beloved community" and schools should strive for this form of community. Dolan in his book on Emerson makes connection between Emerson's thought and King's "beloved community." Dolan cites Emerson's visions of an ideal future society.

> Let our affection flow out to our fellows; it would operate in a day the greatest of all revolutions. It is better to work on institutions by the sun than by the wind. The state must consider every poor man, and all voices must speak for him. Every child that is born must have a just chance for his bread. Let the amelioration of our laws of property proceed from the concession of the rich, not from the grasping of the poor. Let us begin by habitual imparting. (Dolan, pp. 191–192)

Emerson goes on to speak of "renovating the State on the principle of right and love" Dolan then cites Martin Luther King:

> And so at the center of our movement stood the philosophy of love. The attitude that the only way to ultimately change humanity and make for the society that we all long for is to keep love at the center of our lives.... Love in this connection means understanding, redemptive good will ... an overflowing love which is purely spontaneous, unmotivated, groundless and creative.... Whether we call it an unconscious process, an impersonal Brahman, or personal Being of matchless power and infinite love, there is a creative force in

this universe that works to bring the disconnected aspects of reality into a harmonious whole. (Dolan, pp. 192–193)

The Beloved Community is powerful vision for schools which includes justice and love as central principles. Caring, a form of love, has been central to the work of Nel Noddings (1992), who has written extensively about how caring can be a central value and practice in our schools. She suggests that students can learn to care for ourselves, others (both those close to us and people we do not know), plants and animals, and ideas. She offers a comprehensive approach which she summarizes in the following way.

1. Be clear and unapologetic about our goal. The main aim of education should be to produce competent, caring, loving, and lovable people.
2. Take care of affiliative needs.
    a. Keep students and teachers together (by mutual consent) for several years.
    b. Keep students together where possible.
    c. Keep them in the same building for considerable periods of time.
    d. Help students to think of the school as *theirs*.
    e. Legitimize time spent in building relations of care and trust.
3. Relax the impulse to control.
    a. Give teachers and students more responsibility to exercise judgment.
    b. Get rid of competitive grading.
    c. Reduce testing and use a few well-designed tests to assess whether people can handle the tasks they want to undertake competently.
    d. Encourage teachers to explore with students. We do not have to know everything to teach well.
    e. Define expertise more broadly and instrumentally. For example, a biology teacher should be able to teach whatever mathematics is involved in biology.
    f. Encourage self-evaluation.
    g. Involve students in governing their own classrooms and schools.
    h. Accept the challenge to care by teaching well the things students want to learn.
4. Get rid of program hierarchies. This will take time, but we must begin now to provide excellent program for *all* our children. Programs for the noncollege bound should be just as rich, desirable, and rigorous as those for the college bound.

    a. Abandon uniform requirements for college entrance. What a student wants to do or to study should guide what is required by way of preparation.

    b. Give all students what all students need: genuine opportunities to explore the questions central to human life.

5. Give at least part of every day to themes of care.
   a. Discuss existential questions freely, including spiritual matters.
   b. Help students to treat each other ethically. Give them practice in caring.
   c. Help students to understand how groups and individuals create rivals and enemies. Help them to learn how to "be on both sides."
   d. Encourage a way of caring for animals, plants, and the environment that is consistent with caring for humans.
   e. Encourage caring for the human-made world. Help students to be at home in technical, natural, and cultural worlds. Cultivate wonder and appreciation for the human-made world.

6. Teach them that caring in every domain implies competence. When we care, we accept the responsibility to work continuously on our own competence so that the recipient of our care-person, animal, object, or idea—is enhanced. There is nothing mushy about caring. It is the strong, resilient backbone of human life. (pp. 174–175)

The teacher who is authentic and present to students helps build the beloved community. In fact, community must start with the teacher so that students feel safe and cared for in the classrooms and schools.

bell hooks (2000) writes about creating a love ethic which involves "care, commitment, trust, responsibility, respect and knowledge" in our lives (p. 94). Our schools should also work on creating a love ethic. She (1999) speaks directly about love in teaching.

> There is an intimacy in great teaching.... So think first about how you can love your students. Do this even before you think about how you're going to teach them. Think: How can I love these strangers, these others that I see in the classroom? What practice of compassion can I bring to the moment that is so fine-tuned that I can accomplish in one day that which might ordinarily take weeks, months or years to do? (p. 125)

hooks then goes on to advocate meditation as way of developing awareness as vehicle for developing this compassion and love.

EARTH CONNECTIONS

Thoreau's (1961) writing can be a vehicle for connecting to the earth. When he writes about nature there is a strong lyrical quality to this writing.

> I seem to see somewhat more of my own kith and kin in the lichens on the rocks than in any books. It does seem as if mine were a peculiarly wild nature, which so yearns toward all wildness. I know of no redeeming qualities in me but sincere love for some things…. My love is invulnerable. (p. 28)

Thoreau helps us to love the earth. It is through such love that we may be able to stop environmental degradation.

Due to industrialization, competitiveness, and consumerism, we are no longer able to feel or sense the world around us. Thomas Berry (1988) comments:

> We are not even seeing what we are looking at. We are not even smelling the odors that are around us. Our senses are becoming deadened. Such diminishment of our sensitivities kills off our religious sensitivities and diminishes our understanding. It dulls our imagination. I sometimes say, "Don't go to sleep, stay awake, stay awake!" (p. 95)

Holistic education and the ecology movement are closely linked through the concept of interdependence. Both share the principle that interconnectedness is a fundamental reality of nature and should guide our awareness and actions.

Earth connections, then, can reawaken us to the natural processes of life. The wind, the sun, the trees, and grass can help us come alive and awaken us from the treadmill we find ourselves on. As much as possible, students should have direct experiences with the earth through such activities as gardening, caring for animals, and outdoor education. They can also read indigenous peoples literature and others who have written passionately about their relationship to earth. As much as possible, ecological education should arise from a love and reverence for the earth rather from a sense of guilt.

Ojiya School

In Japan, I met a principal, Giichiroi Youmanichi, whose mission was to bring a small forest to the school grounds. One of the schools where he worked was Ojiya school, a large elementary school, which is near Nagaoka, a city that lies in North Western Japan. I have visited this school, but most of my description of the school is based on Ikue Tezuka's (1995) book *School with Forest and Meadow*. There is small forest on the edge of the school grounds. Before the forest was planted students surveyed the surrounding area and identified 96 types of trees and shrubs which were native to the area. After identifying the different types, the students, with the help of teachers and parents, planted 290 trees in an area of approximately 120 square meters.

When planting the trees, the students considered the distribution of tall and short trees and the colors of the buds, flowers, and fruit. Tezuka (1995) comments:

> The result is beautiful to see. Spring is the season of the biggest change. Many of the trees burst forth in buds and blossoms at the same time. In May, the green grows deeper, and the red blossoms are brilliant against the green background. The red azaleas are especially beautiful. From early summer to autumn, the various trees flower one after another with their white, red, and purple flowers. In autumn the trees bend toward the earth under their load of delicious fruit. Then comes the season of autumnal coloring. (p. 8)

The children love watching these changes. They also like to talk to the trees and write poems. Below are some poems written by children in the third grade:

Trees in The Home Forest

Yukari Kazama

I saw trees in the ground.
They are moving as if they were dancing with snow.
Don't they feel heavy
When they have snow on their branches?

Big Red Buds

Rie Nagahashi

Big red buds on a small tree.
They look like candle lights, red candies, cherries, rubies
Big, red, pretty buds.
Nice buds.
They seem to say, "I'm pretty."
(pp. 9–10)

At Ojiya school students develop a bond with the animals and the trees so that they do not see themselves as separate from the environment.

I have met and worked with Yamanouchi and he is one of the most interesting and passionate educators I have ever met. Although he is retired now, he is still very active and extremely energetic. He won an award for his work and a day was held in his honor in June, 2004. My wife and I attended this day where former students and parents commented on the impact of having small forest on the school grounds. One parent got up and talked about how an experience with his daughter at the school had a profound impact on him. One day he went with her to school to look at the tree she was taking care of. There was a small vine growing around the bottom of the tree and the father started to remove it. His daughter got upset and said: "Don't do that! The vine and the tree are friends." The father said that his daughter's words hit him like a hammer and since that moment he has looked on the natural world in a different way. He said he is much more sensitive to the environment in his work in the construction industry.

I believe that Yamanouchi's work is an inspiring example of how students can connect more deeply to the earth and its processes. Of course there are others including the efforts to create gardens on school grounds. (Kiefer and Kemple, 1998).

Cosmic Education

Maria Montessori developed the concept of *cosmic education* that I believe the Transcendentalists would have endorsed. Montessori's son, Mario (1992) describes cosmic education when he writes: "Cosmic education seeks to offer the young, at the appropriate sensitive period, the stimulation and help they need to develop their minds, their vision, and their creative power, whatever the level or range of their personal contributions may be" (p. 101). Her son wrote that the child needs to have a "prior interest in the whole" so he or she can make sense of individual facts. This can be done in part by introducing students to ecological principles that focus on the interdependence of living and nonliving things. Mario Montessori gives the example of students studying the life cycle of salmon and its relationship with the environment.

Aline Wolf (2004) has written about Montessori's vision of cosmic education. She argues that

> Essentially Montessori's cosmic education gives the child first an all-encompassing sense of the universe with its billions of galaxies. Then it focuses on our galaxy, the Milky Way, our solar system, planet Earth and its geological history, the first specimens of life, all species of plants and animals and finally human beings. Inherent in the whole study is the interconnectedness of all creation, the oneness of things. (p. 6)

Wolf also makes reference to the work of Brian Swimme and the Universe story (Swimme, 1992). Cosmic education helps the children place themselves within the total framework of the universe. The image of the universe presented by Montessori and Swimme is one of order and purpose. Since human beings are part of the universe, it gives us a common reference point beyond the boundaries created by nations and religions. Wolf also points out the cosmic education can help children develop a sense of reverence for life and care for the earth. Seeing the miracle of life on earth within the vastness of the universe can help students appreciate more deeply life and the earth itself. Cosmic education can also give students a deep sense of gratitude:

> As examples, when we see a beautiful valley nestled in the mountains, we can reflect on the fact that it was formed by water that labored thousands of years to wear down the mountainous terrain, when we enter a car or train, we can look back and feel grateful to the first human being who constructed a wheel. Awareness of the long-term cosmic pattern, of which we are only an infinitesimal part, calls us to a deep humility and reverence for all the labors of nature and the work of human beings that preceded us (Wolf, p. 16).

Wolf suggests that cosmic education can give children a sense of meaning and purpose in their lives. Montessori felt that within the person lay a *spiritual embryo* which needs to be respected and nourished so that students can eventually find their purpose on earth.

THINKING CONNECTIONS

The Transcendentalists viewed thinking holistically. Emerson (2003) wrote:

> Inquiry leads us to that source, at once the essence of genius, of virtue, and of life, which we call Spontaneity or Instinct. We denote this primary wisdom as Intuition, whilst all later teachings are tuitions. In that deep force, the last fact behind which analysis cannot go, all things find their common origin. (p. 277)

I believe that Fuller's citing of Minerva and Muse as metaphors for the integrated woman, who uses both her intellect and intuition, can be applied to both genders. Likewise what she wrote in *Woman in the Nineteenth Century* is relevant:

> It is with just that hope, that we welcome every thing that tends to strengthen the fiber and develop that nature on more sides. When the intellect and affections are in harmony; when intellectual consciousness is calm and deep; inspiration will not be confounded with fancy. (1992, p. 303)

A holistic approach to thinking incorporates both analysis and intuition. The right brain is home of intuition and the left side is the home analytic thinking. In her book Jill Bolte Taylor (2009), a brain scientist, describes her stroke experience and how it made her aware of the importance of right-brained perception. Her stroke affected her left brain which is the seat of logical thought and language. She refers to this "brain chatter" or that "calculating intelligence that knows when you have to do your laundry" (p. 31). It is also home of our "ego center." The right hemisphere sees things in relationship and in the large context of the whole.

> ... our right mind perceives each of us as equal members of the human family. It identifies our similarities and recognizes our relationship with this marvelous planet, which sustains our life. It perceives the big picture, how everything is related, and how we all join together to make up the whole. Our ability to be empathic, to walk in the shoes of another and feel their feelings is a product of our right frontal cortex. (p. 30)

Taylor also suggests that it is the place where we experience inner peace.... For a time, her life was dominated by the right brain and here she experienced moments of deep peace and feelings of being connected to the cosmos. Before the stroke, like most people living in the industrialized world, Taylor was caught up in "do-do-doing lots of stuff at a very fast pace" (p. 70). This stressful existence also led to frustration and anger. Her stroke allowed her to experience a different world. She writes "In absence of my left hemisphere's negative judgment, I perceived myself as perfect, whole, and beautiful just the way I was" (p. 74).

Through rehabilitation therapy Taylor has recovered the use of her left brain but she has learned to use both sides of the brain to live more fully and realize a deeper happiness. Now when she begins to feel stress she "shifts right" and thus slows down and now listens to her body and trusts her instincts. She breathes deeply and repeats to herself. "*In this moment, I reclaim my JOY, or In this moment I am perfect, whole, and beautiful, or I am an innocent and peaceful child of the universe*, I shift back into the consciousness of right mind" (p. 178).

Our students need to use both the right and left brain. They need to be able to think clearly and analyze information but they also need to see relationships and feel the kind of peace that Taylor and all of us can experience. The Transcendentalists thought holistically and were not afraid to trust their intuitions.

With regard to education, I believe that the use of imagery and metaphor in the classroom can stimulate the right side of the brain while various approaches to critical thinking can support the left side (Miller, 2007). Carl Jung felt that images were symbols coming from the soul and should be honored. One use of imagery is in creative writing. Below is one example from Williams (1983):

> Select a piece of music that evokes strong images for you. Play it for the class (after a relaxation exercise and suitable introduction) and ask them to let the music suggest images, moods, feelings, and sensations to them. Tell them to be receptive to whatever comes to them as the music plays. Afterward, ask them to talk or write about the experience in either prose or poetry. You can start with prose and select the strongest images to form the basis for poetry; or one or two strong images may serve as the basis for a longer prose piece.

This fantasy can also be used as a stimulus for an art project. If you use it for both visual and verbal expression, you might devote some class time to discussing how the experiences differed (some students will prefer writing, others painting; it's a matter of personal style). (p. 133).

Metaphor is also a useful tool in facilitating intuition. Emerson (1990) wrote, "The world is emblematic. Parts of speech are metaphors, because the whole of nature is a metaphor of the human mind" (p. 31). Metaphor not only encourages the student to make connections but to see patterns. For example, in comparing revolutions to volcanoes the student must examine the patterns and principles common to both and then make the connection between the two. Another advantage of the metaphor is that it is open-ended and provokes inquiry. Metaphors by their very nature encourage questions since there are rarely ready-made answers to metaphoric inquiry. For example, in comparing X and Y we first have to inquire into the nature of each and then draw comparisons.

Wilson (2001) argues that metaphors are critical to the learning process and that teachers in working with elementary school children should use metaphorical language in their teaching. Steinbergh (1999) also explores the use of metaphor with elementary school children with a particular focus on poetry. She argues that poetry naturally lends itself to the use of metaphor and the students' ability to use metaphor increases in complexity as they mature. She found that in the primary years metaphors tend to be very concrete as by early adolescence they become more abstract. Using Piaget's developmental framework Flynn (1995) believes that metaphors are best used with students who have reached formal operations. Flynn argues that metaphors can help the student to recall and integrate new concepts. Fleckenstein (1995) works with community college students and describes methods of teaching student writers through the use of metaphor. She argues that these methods help students develop skills of imagination and logical reasoning.

BODY–MIND CONNECTIONS

Thoreau (1961) believed that we need to inhabit our whole bodies. He wrote, "A man thinks as well through his legs and arms as his brain. We exaggerate the importance and exclusiveness of the headquarters.... The poet's words are, "You would almost say the body thought!" I quite say it" (p. 212). Elizabeth Peabody believed that young children must move if they are to develop. She wrote about "Romping, the ecstasy of the body" (Ronda, p. 292).

Holistic education seeks to restore the connection between body and mind; for example, Waldorf education uses eurythmy to maintain this connection. Eurythmy is a unique form of movement education that is usually taught by a teacher trained in the field, but the classroom teacher is encouraged to take part in the lesson. Harwood (1958) suggests: "When the eurythmy teacher is as much interested in what the children are learning in their main lessons, as the class teacher in what they are doing in movement, the children thrive in a harmony of mind and will" (p. 154). In secondary school, eurythmy can be combined with drama, "perhaps in a play when there are nature spirits, as in Milton's *Comus*, or *A Midsummer Night's Dream*" (p. 155). Harwood concludes by emphasizing the importance of eurythmy in Waldorf education:

> Of all elements in modern life it is the rhythmical side which is most defi-cient—a deficiency only too apparent in the arts today. The whole of a Waldorf education is based on rhythm, and may therefore be called curative for an age. But in this rhythmical education there is no doubt where the cen-tre lies. It is in Eurythny (p. 155).

Another vehicle for inhabiting our bodies is mindfulness. Mindfulness is being attentive in the moment; it is being full present to what is happening in the here and now. By being in the moment we inhabit our bodies more fully. Thoreau (2002) wrote about the importance of being present in his essay on walking.

> I am alarmed when it happens that I have walked a mile into the woods bod-ily, without getting there in spirit.... The thought of some work will run in my head and I am not where my body is—I am out of my senses. In my walks I would fain return to my senses. What business have I in the woods, if I am thinking of something out of the woods? (p. 153)

How many times a day do we experience "I am not where my body is"? Emerson (1990) also wrote about being present:

> Since our office is with moments, let us husband them. To finish the moment, to find the journey's end in every step of the road, to live the greatest number of good hours is wisdom....
> Five minutes of today are worth as much to me as five minutes in the next millennium. Let us be poised and wise, and our own, today. (p. 233)

Mindfulness practices in schools has expanded rapidly in recent years (Schoeberlein, 2009; Willard, 2010). Below is an example of a mindful walking activity that could used with students:

> Start with your eyes looking down a few feet ahead of you.
> Stand for a few moments just being aware of your body standing. Let the arms rest at the side. Now focus on your feet. Feel the supporting you and resting on the ground. The attention in this meditation is on the foot as it touches the ground and moves. The movement is slow as you lift the foot and gradually place it on the ground.

Just walk a short distance forward (e.g., 10 for 15 yards) and then turn around. As you turn just stop for a moment before you resume your walking.

It is also possible to label the movements so as you lift the foot you might say to yourself "lifting," then "moving" as you move it and "touching" as it touches the ground again. However, the important thing is to keep the attention focused on the feet and the movements.

At the end of the meditation you can just stand for a few moments being aware of your entire body.

Another activity described by Willard (2010) is called "Belly Breathing."

The easiest way to move the breath into the diaphragm is to place one hand on the chest and one on the belly. This can be done either sitting or lying down. Breathe naturally, and notice which hand moves up and down. Simply try to gently move the breath further down with each breath until it is the belly that is moving up and down. Some people find it helpful to imagine a waterfall carrying the breath downward. (p. 66)

The Willard and Schoberlein books present a variety of mindfulness activities so that both teachers and students can be more present.

SOUL CONNECTIONS

Soul was at the center of Transcendentalism thought; for Emerson (2003) it animated the human being.

The one thing in the world, of value, is the active soul. (p. 230)

Let the breath of new life be breathed by you through the forms already existing. For if once you are alive you shall find they shall become plastic and new. The remedy to their deformity is first soul, and second soul, and evermore soul. (p. 122)

Fuller (1992) saw soul as the main vehicle for women's self-realization.

Let us be wise and not impede the soul. Let her work as she will. Let us have one creative energy, one incessant revelation. Let it take what form it will, and let us not bind it by the past to man or woman, black or white…. Let it be. (p. 298, p. 311)

Holistic education echoes the words of Emerson and Fuller and believes nurturing soul as central to human development. The work of Thomas Moore (1992) has done much to reawaken us to the language and experience of soul. He writes, '"Soul" is not a thing, but a quality or dimension of experiencing life and ourselves. It has to do with depth, value, relatedness, heart, and personal substance' (p. 6). Moore does not use the word in a religious sense and this is important when we think about nourishing the student's soul in public education. I have discussed this aspect of holistic education in my book *Education and the Soul* (2000) and have suggested a "curriculum for the inner life" that includes journal writing, narrative, imagery work, and story telling. In some situations contemplative practices such as meditation can be incorporated and Gina Levete (1995) in the UK has made a strong case for this work.

The strongest connection we can have with students is soul-to-soul. A good example of this process comes from the teaching of Jessica Siegel whose work is described in the book *Small Victories* (Freedman, 1990). Jessica taught at Seward Park High in Manhattan which mostly serves the children of immigrants to the US. In this school of 3,500 students, where the odds seem overwhelming, 92% of the graduates go on to higher education.

Jessica taught English and one of the most important parts of her curriculum was having students write an essay on "Who Am I?" She was not interested in a superficial essay on "What I Did on My Summer Vacation"; instead, she wanted the students to share their thoughts and feelings. There were several benefits to this process. First, she saw how powerful autobiographical essay can help a student get into college or university. For example, one student, Vinnie Mickles, had a 69% average yet was able to get into The State University of New Paltz. Vinnie had never met his biological father and his mother had been in and out of psychiatric hospitals a half-dozen times. He lived in an apartment with his mother where there was no heat and it was so cold that his hands froze and cracked so badly that they bled. The landlord was trying to force out the tenants so that he could raise the rent or sell the building. Because of these conditions, he could not concentrate on his work. Jessica recognized his potential and passed him. He entered the Marine Corps after graduating from Seward. After 2 years in the Corps he came back to Jessica and wanted her help to get into university. Jessica had him write his autobiography and "he delivered a devastatingly dispassionate tale of his mad mother, his absent father, his icy apartment." (p. 48) On the basis of his autobiography Vinnie was accepted at The State University of New York.

After reading autobiographies like Vinnie's, Jessica experiences a strong sense of connection to her students:

> Every year she finishes the autobiographies the same way. Her students are heroes. Her heroes, even some who fail the coursework. Could anyone else understand that? How they fill her with awe. How they, yes, inspire her. (Freedman, p. 68)

Reading these stories allows Jessica's soul to open to the student's soul as expressed in the stories. After reading the stories the students are not just faces in the classrooms but human beings with the uniqueness that comes from soul.

Several educators including Parker Palmer (1998), Rachael Kessler (2000), and Isabella Calillo-Kates (2010) have written about how soul can be nourished in various educational settings including public school classrooms. Kessler in her work focused on how soul can be invited into the classroom through seven gateways: Deep Connection, Meaning and Purpose, Silence, Joy, Creativity, Transcendence and Initiation.

TEACHING WITH SOUL

As I mentioned in the last chapter, holistic education should flow from the soul of the teacher. Unfortunately, educational reform has ignored the teacher's soul with its focus on standardized testing.

In working with teachers and teachers in training for the past 20 years, I have focused on ways to nurture the teacher's soul. I have used contemplative practices as the main vehicle for this process. In my courses for both graduate and pre-service students, I introduce them to six different types of meditation which include: meditation on the breath, counting the breath, lovingkindness (sending thoughts of well being to self and others), mantra (meditation on sound or phrase), movement (e.g., walking), visualization, and contemplation on poetry or sacred texts. Some students work out their own forms and integrate meditation with their own spiritual and religious practice. Although sitting meditation is encouraged, some students do movement meditation. Whatever form students choose, meditation can be seen as *letting go of the calculating mind and opening to the listening mind that tends to be characterized by a relaxed alertness*. Students are asked to meditate each day for 6 weeks. In the beginning, they meditate for about 10–15 min a day and by the end of the 6 weeks they are encouraged to meditate 20–30 min. Students are required to keep a journal which focuses on how the process of meditation is going (e.g., how the concentration and focus are going, how the body is feeling, etc.). The journals also focus on how meditation has affected them. Some of themes have included:

- Giving themselves permission to be alone and enjoy their own company;
- Increased listening capacities;
- Feeling increased energy;
- Being less reactive to situations and generally experiencing greater calm and clarity.

I have also conducted a qualitative study on the longterm impact of the meditation practice on teachers who have been in my courses. (Miller & Nozawa, 2002) This research supported the initial findings from the journal entries.

At the end of the process they write a reflective summary of the experience. Below is an excerpt from one of these summaries speaks to how contemplative practice was nourishing to this woman's being.

> Through meditation I feel that I am being gently invited to observe the nature of my own humanity. Personally I had been strongly moved and transformed through the beautiful nature of this spiritual practice. I had heard my voice and soul with amusement. I had slowly let my inner judge go away and be more in touch with the unspoken, the unseen, and the sacred part of myself. I had achieved a larger vision of my self and my reality, a vision that tenderly dilutes my fears, preconceptions, judgments and need for control. Because of meditation I had been able to transform my fear, anger, and resistance into joy, forgiveness, acceptance and love.
>
> I can bring to meditation anything that is for the purpose of seeing it or feeling it. The reflection and contemplation offered by this practice provides a very safe and comfortable environment where my creativity, intuition, and imagination can be enlarged. I can feel, see, and reflect on my reality while I confess my own fears and personal dilemmas to the being that exists within myself. I become my own witness, my own mentor and my own source of liberation. I can unveil the many layers that cover my real nature so I can then be able to recognize my own needs and inclinations.
>
> Meditating has also been a road of discovering for me. I first discovered the honoring power that the soul possesses for every human being. Through meditation I discovered the unconditional acceptance that is available to the heart of every human being. It is through the practice of meditation that I had better understood the meaning and importance of accepting and honoring myself and others.

Emerson (1966) in his essay about education wrote about teachers using "methods of love" (p. 224). As bell hooks has pointed out, meditation is a way for teachers to love themselves and their students. I have witnessed this transformation in many of the 2000 students I have worked with over the past 20 years. There are many other practices besides meditation that can also nurture soul such as gardening, being in nature, and keeping a gratitude journal. The common factor in these practices is that we move from the calculating mind of the ego to the listening sphere of the soul. This receptive space allows the soul to come forth. In his essay on education Emerson (1966) wrote:

> By simple living by an illimitable soul, you inspire, you correct, you instruct, you raise, you embellish all. By your own act you teach the beholder how to do the practicable. According to the depth from which you draw your life, such is the depth not only of your strenuous effort, but of your manners and presence. (p. 227)

My experience of introducing contemplative practices to teachers is that these practices provide the "depth" that Emerson refers to and are instrumental in enhancing the presence of the teacher in the classroom.

CONCLUSION

There is a public school in Toronto called The Equinox Holistic Alternative School (formerly called The Whole Child School) that uses the connections outlined above as the framework for the curriculum (see their website www.wholechildschool.ca for the link—The Holistic Curriculum). This framework has allowed them to incorporate ideas from various sources such as Montessori and Waldorf education without being limited by the confines of one approach. I have described the school in more detail in my book *Whole Child Education*. They have incorporated many of ideas described in this book. For example, there is a strong focus on environmental education and the Kindergarten program occurs mostly outdoors. The connection to Thoreau's vision is evident throughout the curriculum. There is also a strong emphasis on integrated curriculum as themes are used to connect subjects such as science and math.

As noted in the preface, the Transcendentalists are part of a long tradition where education nurtures whole human beings and connects them to community, the earth and the universe. Still, there are a few caveats when one tries to apply the ideas of the Transcendentalists to holistic education today. The first concern would be nineteenth century language which, of course, is not gender neutral. We can also find it difficult to relate to phrases such as "Riding the Chariots of Glory" that Alcott used in his senior years. In a post—nuclear age of uncertainty, readers today may also take issue with the idea of a "Universal Intelligence" that Thoreau and Emerson wrote about. However, this latter issue is not limited to Transcendental Learning since the idea of such an intelligence can also be linked to Montessori education and Waldorf education which continue to grow and expand around the world. Like Montessori and Steiner, I believe the Transcendentalists can inspire educators but there is always the danger that some will want to try follow their ideas too closely rather using them as a touchstone. Their work should encourage us to look within and trust our own intuitions and so we can "build our own world." Emerson wrote that the poet is "free and they make free." Like the poet, the teacher should also "be free and make free."

REFERENCES

Beane, J. (1997). *Curriculum integration: Designing the core of democratic education*. New York: Teachers College Press.

Berry, T. (1988). *Dream of the earth*. San Fransisco, CA: Sierra Book Club.

Colalillo-Kates, I. & Harvey, C. L. (Eds.). (2010). *The wheels of soul in education: An inspiring international dynamic*. Rotterdam: Sense.

Dolan, N. (2009). *Emerson's liberalism*. Madison, WI: University of Wisconsin Press.

Drake, S. (1998). *Creating integrated curriculum.* Thousand Oaks, CA: Corwin.

———— (2007). *Creating standards based integrated curriculum.* Thousand Oaks, CA: Corwin.

Emerson, R. W. (1990). *Selected essays, lectures, and poems.* New York, NY: Bantam.

Emerson, R. W. (2003). *Selected writings of Ralph Waldo Emerson.* New York, NY: Signet.

Fleckenstein, K. (1995, May). "Writing and the strategic use of metaphor." *Teaching English in the Two-year College, 22,* 110–115.

Flynn, L. (1995, Winter). "Learning concepts independently through metaphor." *Reading Improvement, 32,* 200–219.

Freedman, S. (1990). *Small victories: The real world of a teacher, her students & their high school.* New York, NY: Harper & Row.

Fuller, Margaret. (1992). *The Essential Margaret Fuller.* Jeffrey Steele (Ed.). New Brunswick, NJ: Rutgers University Press.

Gallegos Nava, R. (2001). *Holistic education: Pedagogy of universal love.* Brandon, VT: Foundation of Educational Renewal.

Harwood, A. C. (1958). *The recovery of man in childhood: A study in the educational work of Rudolf Steiner.* Spring Valley, NY: Anthroposophic Press.

hooks, b. (2000). *All about love: New visions.* New York, NY: HarperPerennial.

Kessler, R. (2000). *The soul of education: Helping students find connection, compassion, and character at school.* Alexandria, VA: ASCD.

Kiefer, J., & Kemple, M. (1998). *Digging deeper: Integrating youth gardens into schools & communities.* Montpelier, VT: Foodworks.

Levete, G. (1995). *Presenting the case for meditation in primary and secondary schools.* London: Interlink Trust.

Miller, J. (2000). *Education and the soul: Toward a spiritual curriculum.* Albany, NY: SUNY Press.

Miller, J., & Nozawa A. (2002). Meditating teachers: A qualitative study. *Journal of Inservice Education, 28,* 179–192.

———— (2007). *The holistic curriculum.* Toronto: University of Toronto Press.

———— (2010). *Whole child education.* Toronto: University of Toronto Press.

Moore, T. (1992). *Care of the soul: A guide for cultivating depth and sacredness in everyday life.* New York, NY: Walker & Co.

Palmer, P. (1998). *The courage to teach.* San Francisco, CA: Jossey-Bass.

Noddings, N. (1992). *The challenge to care in schools: An alternative approach to education.* New York, NY: Teachers College Press.

Ronda, B. A. (1999). *Elizabeth Palmer Peabody: A reformer on her own terms.* Cambridge, MA: Harvard University Press.

Schoeberlein, D. (2009). *Mindful teaching and Teaching mindfulness.* Boston, MA: Wisdom.

Steinbergh, J. (1999). Mastering metaphor through poetry. *Language arts,* March, 76, 231–234.

Swimme, B. & Berry, T. (1992). *The universe story.* San Francisco, CA: Harper Collins.

Taylor, J. B. (2009). *My stroke of insight: A brain scientist's personal journey.* New York, NY: Plume.

Tezuka, I. (1995). *School with forest and meadow.* San Francisco, CA: Caddo Gap Press.

Thoreau, H. D. (1961). Shepard, O. (Ed.), *The heart of Thoreau's journals*. New York, NY: Dover.

Thoreau, H. D. (2002). *The essays of Henry D. Thoreau*. L. Hyde (Ed.). New York, NY: North Point Press.

Willard, C. (2010). *Child's mind: Mindfulness practices to help our children be more focused, calm and relaxed*. Berkeley, CA: Parallax Press.

Williams, L. V. (1983). *Teaching for the two-sided mind*. Englewood Cliffs, NJ: Prentice Hall.

Wilson, S. L. A. (2001). "A metaphor is pinning air to the wall": A literature review of children's use of metaphor. *Childhood Education, 77*(2), 96–99.

Wolf, A. (2004). "Maria Montessori cosmic education as a non-sectarian framework for nurturing children's spirituality." Pacific Grove, CA: ChildSpirit Conference, October 7–10.

Note: Noddings quotation.

SUGGESTED READINGS

TRANSCENDENTALISM

Bickman, M. (2003). *Minding American education: Reclaiming the tradition of active learning*. New York, NY: Teachers College Press.
This is an excellent text which examines the work of the Transcendentalists, William James, and John Dewey.

Buell, L. (2006). *The American transcendentalists: Essential writings*. New York, NY: Penguin. pp. xi–xxiii.
An excellent collection of papers by the Transcendentalists covering wide range of subjects.

Gura, P. F. (2007). *American transcendentalism: A history*. New York, NY: Hill and Wang.
The best overall history of Transcendentalism.

Hawken, P. (2007). *Blessed Unrest: How the largest movement in the world came into being and why no one saw it coming*. New York, NY: Viking.
This book shows the legacy of Emerson and Thoreau today in what Hawken calls the "movement without a name."

Howe, D. W. (2007). *What hath God wrought: The transformation of America, 1815–1848*. New York, NY: Oxford.
A Pulitzer Prize winning overview of this period which includes a section on the Transcendentalists.

TRANCENDENTALISTS

Alcott, A. Bronson. (1991). *How like an angel came I down: Conversations with children on the Gospels*. A. O. Howell (Ed.). Hudson, NY: Lindisfarne Press.
Alcott's conversations with students at the Temple School.

Capper, C. (2002). *Margaret Fuller: An American romantic Life. The private years*. New York, NY: Oxford University Press.
First of a two volume biography of Fuller which contains chapters on her teaching career.

Emerson, R. W. (2003). *Selected writings of Ralph Waldo Emerson*. New York, NY: Signet.
The introduction by Afro-American scholar, Charles Johnson, shows the relevance of Emerson's thought. This collection includes Emerson's essay on Education.

Fuller, M. (1992). *The essential Margaret Fuller*. Jeffrey Steele (Ed.). New Brunswick, NJ: Rutgers University Press.
A collection of her writings including *Woman in the Nineteenth Century*.

Gruenewald, D. A. (2002). Teaching and learning with Thoreau, *The Harvard Educational Review. 72*, 515–539.
This paper explores Thoreau's ideas on education and their relevance for education today.

Harding, W. (1982). *The days of Henry Thoreau: A biography*. New York, NY: Dover.
This biography contains excellent descriptions of Thoreau's teaching experiences.

Marshall, M. (2005). *The Peabody sisters: Three women who ignited American romanticism*. Boston: Houghton Mifflin.
This book contains material on Elizabeth Peabody's early teaching career.

Matteson, John. (2007). *Eden's outcasts: The story of Louis May Alcott and her Father*. New York, NY: W. W. Norton.
A Pulitzer Prize winning biography of the two Alcotts.

Peabody, E. P. (1845). *The Record of a school. Exemplifying the general principles of spiritual culture*. Bedford, MA: Applewood Books.
This books describes the Temple School and is a classic in the field of holistic education.

Richardson, R. D. (1995). *Emerson: The mind on fire*. Berkeley, CA: University of California Press.
An excellent biography of Emerson.

Ronda, B. A. (1999). *Elizabeth Palmer Peabody: A reformer on her own terms*. Cambridge, MA: Harvard University Press.
This biography which describes Peabody as a 'practical intellectual" and her long career as an educator.

Thoreau, H. D. (1986). *Walden and civil disobedience*. New York, NY: Penguin.
A classic in American literature.

HOLISTIC EDUCATION

Gallegos Nava, Ramon. (2001). *Holistic education: Pedagogy of universal love*. Brandon, VT: Foundation for Educational Renewal.
This book discusses the theoretical foundations for holistic education.

Kessler, R. (2000). *The soul of education: Helping students find connection, compassion and character at school*. Alexandria, VA: Association for Supervision and Curriculum Development.
Based on years of classroom experience, Kessler shows how the soul can be nourished in the public school classroom.

Miller, J. P. (2000). *Education and the soul: Toward a spiritual curriculum*. Albany, NY: SUNY press.
This book explores the concept of soul and how it can be nurtured through a curriculum for the inner life as well through experiences in nature and art.

Miller, J. P. (2010). *Whole child education*. Toronto: University of Toronto Press.
This book describes basic features of holistic education and how it has been implemented in one school in Toronto.

Miller, R. (1997). *What are schools for? Holistic education in American culture*. Brandon VT: Holistic Education Press.
Excellent historical treatment of holistic education and includes a section on the Transcendentalists.

Palmer, P. J. (1998). *The courage to teach: Exploring the inner landscape of the teacher's life*. San Francisco, CA: Jossey-Bass.
This book has become a classic in the field of spirituality in education and explains how teachers can live the "undivided life."

ABOUT THE AUTHOR

John (Jack) Miller has been working in the field of holistic education for over 30 years. He is author/editor of more than a dozen books on holistic learning and contemplative practices in education, which include *Education and the Soul, Educating for Wisdom and Compassion, The Holistic Curriculum,* and most recently, *Whole Child Education*. His writing has been translated into eight languages. The *Holistic Curriculum* has provided the framework for the curriculum at the Whole Child School, now named the Equinox Holistic Alternative School, in Toronto where Jack has served on the Advisory Board.

Jack has worked extensively with holistic educators in Japan, Korea, and Hong Kong for the past 15 years and has been a visiting professor at universities in Japan and Hong Kong. In 2009, Jack was one of 24 educators invited to Bhutan to help that country develop their educational system so that it supports the country's goal of Gross National Happiness. He teaches courses on holistic education and spirituality in education for graduate students and students in Initial Teacher Education Program at the Ontario Institute for Studies in Education at the University of Toronto where he is Professor.

INDEX